TRAVELLERS

CARIBBEAN
CRUISING

By
EMMA STANFORD

Written by Emma Stanford, updated by Polly Thomas

Published by Thomas Cook Publishing
A division of Thomas Cook Tour Operations Limited.
Company registration no. 1450464 England
The Thomas Cook Business Park, Unit 9, Coningsby Road,
Peterborough PE3 8SB, United Kingdom
Email: books@thomascook.com, Tel: + 44 (0) 1733 416477
www.thomascookpublishing.com

Produced by Cambridge Publishing Management Limited
Burr Elm Court, Main Street, Caldecote CB23 7NU

ISBN: 978-1-84157-953-5

© 2003, 2006 Thomas Cook Publishing
This third edition © 2008
Text © Thomas Cook Publishing
Maps © Thomas Cook Publishing

Series Editor: Maisie Fitzpatrick
Production/DTP: Steven Collins

Printed and bound in Italy by Printer Trento

Cover photography: All © Thomas Cook

The paper used for this book has been independently certified as having
been sourced from well-managed forests and recycled wood or fibre
according to the rules of the Forest Stewardship Council.
This book has been printed and bound in Italy by Printer Trento S.r.l.,
an FSC certified company for printing books on FSC mixed paper in
compliance with the chain of custody and on products labelling standards.

FSC
Mixed Sources
Product group from well-managed
forests and recycled wood or fibre

Cert no. CQ-COC-000012
www.fsc.org
© 1996 Forest Stewardship Council

Contents

KEY TO MAPS

✈ Airport

D23 (838) (1) Road number

★ Start of walk/tour

1424m ▲ Mountain

/ Country border

Introduction

Since 1492, when Christopher Columbus set off to sail the oceans in search of a western route to the spice islands of the East Indies, travellers have been captivated by the Caribbean. While Columbus signally failed to locate either the Asian mainland or any spices save pepper, he did discover a chain of alluring sun-drenched islands set in azure seas.

He called them the West Indies, a name which has stuck, though the term 'Caribbean' is more accurate, being derived from the Carib Indians encountered by the early explorers. But one thing is for sure, the West Indies-cum-Caribbean still offers a little bit of heaven on earth to visitors from colder climes.

The majority of Caribbean cruises begin from the world's two busiest cruise-ship terminals in Florida (a holiday hotspot in its own right): the Port of Miami, and Port Everglades, in Fort Lauderdale. And there can be no doubt that in the region cruising is the ultimate form of travel. Liberated from transport and luggage hassles, and dining dilemmas, cruise passengers can truly relax and enjoy their vacation.

For some this may extend no further than enjoying a tall glass of Planter's Punch and a good book while on the pool deck. But part of the fun of Caribbean cruising is the

WHERE TO GO

This guide does not attempt to cover every island in the Caribbean region, or even every corner of the islands listed, as more remote spots are usually inaccessible to cruise passengers with limited time. However, in addition to sections devoted to the main Caribbean cruise embarkation ports of Miami and Fort Lauderdale, you'll find entries covering the top cruise-ship ports of call and accessible local attractions on more than 30 Caribbean islands, plus Bermuda, a summer season favourite in the Atlantic Ocean, and Key West, a US mainland stop on several cruise routes.

variety of destinations visited in a short period of time. Wake up each morning with a new group of islands on the horizon and a different port at the foot of the gangplank . . . and realise that somebody else has done all the work!

Every island has its own special flavour. Colonial history may be revealed in architecture, as in the toy-town Dutch gables of Curaçao, or there may be distinctive culinary influences such as the curries of Trinidad and French-Creole dishes of Martinique. There's an island to suit all tastes and budgets from super-chic St Barts to mellow Grenada, the elegant plantation hotels of Nevis to the eardrum-shattering Sunday afternoon reggae sessions atop Shirley Heights in Antigua.

At the end of the day, sightseers and sunseekers alike can enjoy the sunset fanned by a cooling breeze as the ship gets under way, and partake of a gourmet dinner and a spot of entertainment before a stroll on the deck beneath the starry skies.

'Every one of the islands has, for me, its own special scent . . . islands like Grenada or St Vincent float in a subtle aroma of spices.'
DANE CHANDOS
Isles to Windward, 1955

'The West Indies I behold Like the Hesperides of old – Trees of life with fruits of gold.'
JAMES MONTGOMERY
A Voyage Around the World, 1841

Glorious technicolour sunsets are a Caribbean speciality

The land

The flat swampy Florida peninsula emerged from the sea around 20 to 30 million years ago. Its porous limestone base was formed by massive deposits of sediment packed in deep trenches between extinct underwater volcanoes. The Bermuda archipelago, over 1,600km (1,000 miles) out into the Atlantic Ocean, also has limestone underpinnings, and can claim the world's most northerly coral reefs, thanks to the warm waters of the Gulf Stream.

To the south and east of Florida, the dozens of islands and tiny cays (small flat islets, pronounced 'keys') which make up the Bahama Islands reach down towards the Caribbean region which balances somewhat precariously on the rift between the Atlantic and Caribbean tectonic plates.

The Caribbean Islands – more than 7,000 of them, ranging in size from Cuba (110,851sq km/42,800sq miles) to tiny coral atolls just peeking above sea level – begin with Cuba (144km/90 miles off Key West), at the northern extent of the Caribbean Sea. Collectively known as the Antilles, they

The Pitons du Carbet rise above Fort-de-France, Martinique

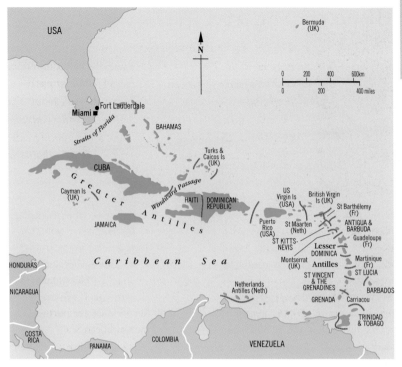

stretch in an arc almost 4,023km (2,500 miles) long, and are split into two main groupings: the Greater Antilles (Cuba to Puerto Rico) in the north; and the Lesser Antilles (Virgin Islands to Trinidad) trailing south towards the coast of Venezuela. A further distinction within the Lesser Antilles is made between the Windward Islands (which receive the brunt of the trade winds off the Atlantic) and the Leeward Islands.

Caribbean scenery varies dramatically from island to island. The mountainous uplands of Jamaica or Puerto Rico could not be a greater contrast to the low-lying limestone and coral Cayman Islands, or the Dutch Leewards with their spaghetti Western-style cacti and tortured-looking *divi-divi* trees. Nowhere are the region's volcanic origins more obvious than in the imposing, jungle-clad volcanic cones of the Windward Islands. Several Windward volcanoes are still active, and visitors can witness steaming, sulphurous (and smelly) volcanic activity in Dominica, St Lucia, Guadeloupe, Martinique and St Vincent. Conditions also differ between the windward (Atlantic) and leeward (Caribbean) sides of the islands. While the rocky coastline of the former is pounded by Atlantic rollers, the sandy strands of the latter are lapped by gentle waves and protected by offshore reefs.

History

1000 BC	First Amerindian tribes, the Ciboney, move to the Caribbean islands from South America.
AD 120	Peaceable fishing and farming Arawak Indians arrive (also from South America).
800	Warlike Carib Indians begin to push the Arawaks from the Lesser Antilles.
1492	12 October: Columbus makes landfall in the Bahamas at San Salvador.
1493–6	Columbus' second voyage sights Dominica, Guadeloupe, Jamaica and Puerto Rico.
1498–1500	Columbus' third voyage adds Grenada, Trinidad and St Vincent.
1502–4	Columbus' fourth voyage reaches the Central American mainland.
1503	Juan Bermudez of Spain sights Bermuda.
1513	Juan Ponce de León steps ashore in Florida, and names the land after the date of his arrival, La Florida, the Spanish Eastertide Feast of Flowers.
1536	Pedro a Campo of Portugal lands on Barbados.
1565	The Spanish create the settlement of St Augustine, Florida.
1600s	'Golden Age' of Caribbean piracy with looting on the high seas. Sugar cane is introduced to the Lesser Antilles; West African slaves are shipped in to work the plantations.
1627	The English settle Barbados.
1648	The French and Dutch divide St Martin/Sint Maarten.
1655	The English seize Jamaica from Spain.
1671	Denmark colonises St Thomas.
1692	The pirate town of Port Royal, Jamaica, destroyed by an earthquake.

1756–63	The Seven Years War leads to Franco-British tussles in the West Indies.
1814–15	West Indies carved up following the Treaties of Paris at the end of the Napoleonic Wars. Britain grabs the lion's share; the French retain Martinique and Guadeloupe; Cuba, Puerto Rico and half of Hispaniola go to Spain; the Dutch and the Danes divide up the rest.
1819	The Spanish relinquish Florida to the USA.
1834	The Emancipation Act abolishes slavery in Britain and its colonies.
1845	Florida achieves statehood. The First East Indian indentured labourers arrive in Trinidad.
1848–63	The French and then the Dutch abolish slavery in their colonies.
1868	Rebuilding of southern USA after the Civil War results in voting rights for Florida's male citizens, including black people.
1880s	Railroads open up Florida.
1896	Henry Flagler's railroad reaches Miami (and Key West in 1912).
1898	Cuba becomes an independent republic, under a spell of US military occupation, and Puerto Rico is ceded to the USA.
1902	Mont Pelée erupts in Martinique and destroys the town of St-Pierre with 30,000 casualties.
1917	The USA purchases the Virgin Islands of St Croix, St John, and St Thomas from Denmark for $25 million. Puerto Ricans receive US citizenship.
1920s	The Florida Land Boom – plots of land sell for fortunes. The market finally collapses with the 1929 Wall Street Crash.
1959	Socialist revolution in Cuba led by Fidel Castro and Ernesto 'Che' Guevara. Castro is elected Prime Minister. Mass exodus of refugees to Miami.
1961	The abortive Bay of Pigs invasion of Cuba by USA-backed anti-Communist exiles.

History

1962   The Cuban Missile Crisis – attempts by the USSR to station nuclear missiles in Cuba are challenged by President John F Kennedy. The Russians back down. Jamaica gains independent statehood. Trinidad and Tobago become a presidential republic.

1966   Barbados achieves independence from Britain.

1971   Walt Disney World® opens in Orlando with the Magic Kingdom®, followed by the EPCOT® Center (1983) and Disney's Hollywood™ Studios (1989).

1974   Grenada gets independent statehood.

1978   Dominica gains independence.

1979   St Lucia, St Vincent and the Grenadines become independent states.

1981   Antigua and Barbuda gain independence.

1983   St Kitt's and Nevis become independent. A US–Eastern Caribbean force 'invades' Grenada to end the socialist regime.

1993   Puerto Rico votes against US statehood, but for association with the USA.

1994   A US 'friendly' invasion reinstates Haiti's deposed President Aristide, but he is voted out in 1995.

1995   Hurricane Luis causes considerable damage in St Martin/Sint Maarten and other islands of the Caribbean.

1997   Montserrat's Soufrière volcano erupts, destroying the capital, Plymouth.

1998   Nevis fails in bid to separate from St Kitts.

2001   Trinidad-born V S Naipaul wins Nobel Prize for Literature.

2005   Florida and the Caribbean are ravaged by a record number of tropical storms and hurricanes.

2007   The Caribbean hosts the ICC Cricket World Cup.

2008   Fidel Castro resigns as Cuba's President in favour of his brother Raúl after nearly 50 years as the nation's leader.

Politics

The Caribbean's deeply fragmented political scene has done nothing to assist the region's overall economic and social situation. Several attempts at providing the framework for a united front have dissolved into unseemly squabbles as the various participants seek to preserve their identity and interests.

After more than four centuries of European domination, the Caribbean islands began to break free of their colonial shackles in the 1950s and 1960s. The majority opted for full independence, but exceptions include the Crown Colonies of the British Virgin Islands, Cayman Islands, Bermuda, the Netherlands Antilles (though not Aruba, which is autonomous), and the French islands of Martinique and Guadeloupe, which are overseas Territories of France.

The United States also wields considerable influence in the region with its interests in the US Virgin Islands (USVI) and Puerto Rico. The USVI (St Thomas, St Croix and St John) are an unincorporated Territory of the USA with a self-elected Senate and Governor, and non-voting delegate to the US House of Representatives.

Puerto Rico is a Commonwealth of the USA, linked to the federal banking system, with an American-style government model. One issue dominates current Puerto Rican politics: whether the island remains a Commonwealth, or opts for statehood.

CARICOM (the Caribbean Common Market), set up in 1973, has had its eye on the cruise-ship industry, which many see as a threat to the all-important tourist trade. CARICOM's response has been to levy higher taxes on cruise ships, but this has not given any meaningful relief to the tourist industry. The immediate problem of waste dumping at sea by cruise ships has been met with draconian (and fully deserved) fines.

The Legislature of the US Virgin Islands, Charlotte Amalie

Culture

Like the product of any great melting pot, Caribbean culture is the sum of its ingredients – and the recipe, in this case, is deliciously exotic. Take a pinch of Spanish influence, a generous measure of French élan and British cool, add a peck of Dutch and Danish, a dash of Portuguese and American, then season generously with West African rhythm and Indian spice – et voilà!

Architecture

A hybrid to the core, Caribbean architecture is both varied and colourful. As a rule, the islands' colonial masters imported techniques from the home country and adapted them to suit the heat.

So, for example, you'll find the sturdy stone Georgian buildings of ex-British St Kitt's and Antigua adorned with louvred shutters and shady balconies. There is a wealth of pretty fretwork decoration, too. Commonly known as 'gingerbread', these carved wooden frills and curlicues adorn porches, gables and eaves right around the West Indies. And they are also popular in Key West, where they were introduced by the Bahamanian migrants around the turn of the 20th century.

Willemstad's picture-postcard Dutch-gabled waterfront houses on Curaçao are daubed in brilliant pastel shades, a custom which supposedly originated when a 19th-century governor declared the combination of brilliant sunshine and whitewash was giving him migraines. In other cases, bits of the 'old country' were simply transplanted wholesale to the New World, such as the cobbled streets of Puerto Rico's Old San Juan, which are as Spanish as *paella*.

Language

English is the unofficial language of the tourist industry throughout the Caribbean, though it might not help much in the French islands of Guadeloupe and Martinique. Although French is also the official language of St Barts and St Martin, English is understood. Again, Spanish is the first language of Puerto Rico but English is widely spoken. The everyday language used by the islanders is *patois*, which may seem comprehensible at first (particularly if you speak some French), but then dissolves into what sounds like gibberish the minute you think you understand. The most common form of *patois* is Creole, a mixture of French and West African laced with occasional English words. If you visit the Dutch Leeward Islands, listen out for Papiamento, a truly baffling combination of English, French, Dutch, Spanish, Portuguese, African and Amerindian elements, developed as a means of communication among 17th-century sailors, slave traders and merchants of all nations.

Music

Music is the heartbeat of the Caribbean. From Trinidadian calypso to Jamaican reggae, you will find its infectious rhythms are as much a part of the Caribbean experience as palm trees and Planter's Punch. If you get the chance to attend any of the springtime pre-Lenten carnivals or summertime 'cropover' festivals celebrating the end of harvest, do not miss out.

There are singing and dancing competitions throughout the year, and spontaneous outbursts of both as part of outdoor 'jump-ups'. Visit the Caribbean at Christmas time and you will be treated to calypso and reggae versions of all your favourite carols, too (*see pp134–5*).

Religion

Since the earliest European settlers arrived, Christianity has been the official religion of the Caribbean, and many of the oldest surviving buildings are churches. As a rough guide, the former Spanish and French islands are Catholic; the numerous old churches on British islands are generally Protestant with a high quota of Baptist and Methodist worshippers. Some African animist traditions (basically, the belief that natural objects possess souls) have also survived in Caribbean superstitions such as the *jumbie* or *duppie* (restless ghost) figures which appear at carnival time.

Rastafarianism has spread from Jamaica, where it first appeared in the 1930s as an offshoot of the peaceful black pride movement. Turning away from Western culture, young West Indians looked to their African roots for a new religious and cultural identity. True Rastas are God-fearing types, both vegetarian and teetotal. Cultural identity is expressed through reggae music, the use of *ganja* (marijuana) to gain spiritual wisdom and the sporting of *rasta* (or dread) locks to represent the natural glory of the lion's mane (one title of their former spiritual leader, Emperor Haile Selassie of Ethiopia, was the 'Conquering Lion of Judah').

Spanish-Catholic heritage in Puerto Rico

Carnival

The explosion of colour, music, singing and dance that is the Caribbean carnival actually has its roots in medieval Europe. The very word 'carnival' is derived from the Italian *carnevale*, which means the removal of meat, and refers to the Christian practice of Lenten abstinence in the period before Easter. The Europeans brought carnival to the New World, notably the Spanish and the French Catholic

Costumes are essential ingredients of the carnival scene...

planters who decamped to Trinidad as revolutionary unrest hit the French possessions at the end of the 18th century.

Between Christmas and Ash Wednesday, the French settlers indulged in a hectic season of parties and masked balls or masquerades, which, shortened to 'Mas', is still a commonly used Trinidadian term for the street parades of costume bands during carnival. With Emancipation in 1838, and the lifting of laws prohibiting slave gatherings and drumming, the former slaves celebrated their freedom every August with processions, took to the streets for fun at Christmas, and before long, hijacked the pre-Lenten Mardi Gras. The result was a fusion of West African and European traditions where folklore performances partnered stilt-riding *moko-jumbies* (make-believe spirits) with characters straight out of biblical tales, and stately quadrilles or waltzes were revamped to an African beat. The emergence of calypso in the 19th century and steel bands in the 1940s (*see p135*) set a truly Caribbean seal on the event. Today, costume bands of thousands of revellers dance through the streets to the strains of soca music pumped from speaker-laden trucks.

Trinidad is still the home of Caribbean carnival (*see p132*), but

...and are often elaborate and colourful

every island has its own version. Some, like Bahamanian Junkanoo, are held over the Christmas period, while July and August see the Cropover (harvest) and Emancipation carnivals on many islands, with the celebration in Barbados being the biggest.

Impressions

A cruising holiday offers, above all else, a trouble-free package which relieves you from the daily hassle of planning and travel while giving you more time to get out there and enjoy yourself. Once you check in your luggage on the dockside you won't have to lug another heavy suitcase until you leave. Life on the ocean wave is a ball, where daily excursions and evening entertainment are all laid on. All you have to do is simply turn up, kick back and relax.

Naturally, your first step is to choose the right cruise and you will find some helpful hints on pages 176–9. But for first-time cruisers, here are a few tips on finding your sea legs.

All aboard!

Embarkation is usually the most gruelling part of any cruise, particularly if you have had a long flight to reach your departure point. Where possible, it is always best to arrange airport transfers with the cruise line through your travel agent.

When you check in, the staff will check your ticket and identification. Your passport or ID may be taken into safekeeping to be returned at the end of your trip. After a brief photo call for the ship's photographer, a steward will escort you to your cabin. Make sure everything is in order. Register any complaints immediately.

Who's who?

Your cruise ship will be run by the 'crew' under the command of the captain. With the exception of the captain himself, who may appear at official drinks parties, and hosts the much sought-after Captain's Table in the dining room, the crew are largely invisible from the passenger's point of view. It is the ship's 'staff' who provide the passenger contact. They include: the chief purser, who is in charge of currency exchange and other money matters; the cruise director and his team of assistants, who oversee shipboard social activities and entertainment; and the shore excursion director. Larger ships may have a hotel manager to oversee the dining and housekeeping functions. Otherwise, these responsibilities lie with the chief steward, who is head of the catering and restaurant facilities, and is assisted by the *maître d'hôtel* in the dining room. The chief housekeeper marshals the cabin stewards and stewardesses, and organises laundry and cleaning services.

The Bahamas are well geared for tourism

Dining and table allocations

In addition to informal self-service eating areas on board ship, all three main meals of the day are served in the more formal dining room. Seating allocations are usually only made for the evening meal – you may specify early or late sittings, smoking or non-smoking section, and details of any special dietary requirements. If you are unhappy with your allotted table, ask for a change.

Spending money

Most cruise lines include in the price of your ticket five meals a day (alcoholic drinks excluded), room service, live entertainment and the use of facilities such as the health club and library. However, remember to budget for additional expenses such as shore excursions, bar bills, laundry, in-room movies, yoga or pilates classes, spa treatments and staff tips at the end of the cruise (*see p188*).

Land ahoy!

Emerging from the air-conditioned comfort of your cruise ship on to a bustling Caribbean dockside can be a bit of a shock in more ways than one. First, there's the heat – so make sure you are comfortably dressed for it. Second, there may be a sea of apparently predatory taxi drivers and hawkers clamouring for your attention. This is not meant to be as intimidating as it seems. A smile and a firm 'no thank you' is a far more potent crowd dissolver than bluster and outrage.

SEASICKNESS

Seasickness is nowadays a rare occurrence owing to highly effective ships' stabilisers and the Caribbean's usual glassy calm, but it is still a possibility for a few unlucky cruisers.

Over-the-counter tablets, such as Dramamine, are available from the ship's stores. Consult the ship's doctor if the queasy feeling continues or if you are taking other medication.

Some motion sickness sufferers prefer acu-pressure wristbands to drugs. For a mild case, take a walk on deck in the fresh air, and focus on a fixed point such as the horizon.

You may, on the other hand, need the services of a taxi driver. Getting around the islands in a limited period of time can be a problem, and the answer is generally a knowledgeable local driver. Before you take a taxi, check out the government or tourist office recommended rates for trips to various popular destinations. They are usually posted in the local tourist office, information booth, or on the dockside itself. This way you can fix the fare in advance, and be sure you are paying a fair rate.

There may be plenty of hustle and bustle on the streets, but Caribbean islanders are never in a hurry. 'Re-l-a-a-a-a-x' is the motto hereabouts, and there is always time for a friendly greeting before any business gets done. This is no place for getting uptight, so slip down a gear or two and enjoy the laid-back attitude. But do not lose grip of your valuables. Though there is little danger of violent crime on most islands, petty theft is a constant irritant.

Cruise ship anchored at Charlotte Amalie, St Thomas

Greater Miami

Cruise port Capital of the World, Miami is the gateway to the Caribbean, a cosmopolitan oceanfront city just a day trip away from the sunny Bahamas Islands. It is a lively, modern metropolis, full of contrasts, cultural diversity and a whole host of tourist attractions and activities. Today, tourism is the city's number one industry, with about 11 million visitors a year. And around three million of these visitors will sail off into the sunset on board one of the 20 or so cruise ships which call the Port of Miami home.

Tourism in Miami began with the arrival of Henry Flagler's railroad in 1896. Florida folklore tells how Yankee pioneer Julia Tuttle intrigued Flagler by sending him fresh Miami orange blossom untouched by the Great Frost of 1894–5, which destroyed citrus groves as far south as Palm Beach. Flagler recognised the tourism potential of such a mild climate, extended his railroad south, and thus founded modern Miami.

During the early years of the 20th century, a handful of wealthy visitors established winter homes along the shore of Biscayne Bay. The grandest of these is James Deering's magnificent Vizcaya.

Then, inspired by the 1920s Florida land boom, George Merrick laid out America's first planned community, Coral Gables, which remains some of the most sought-after real estate in town. Meanwhile, a failed offshore avocado plantation was anchored to the mainland by causeways, and transformed into legendary Miami Beach.

Greater Miami covers a vast area of around 5,283sq km (2,040sq miles). At its heart, the skyscrapers of downtown Miami's business district provide a futuristic skyline. But surprising pockets of early 20th-century charm also exist within the sprawling metropolis. These unexpected treats are often referred to as 'the neighbourhoods'.

The most famous is the pastel-painted Art Deco District on Miami Beach. Mainland Coconut Grove exudes a Bohemian air, while neighbouring Coral Gables boasts Mediterranean-style architecture, country clubs and tree-shaded avenues.

For local colour, look no further than the bustling Cuban district of Little Havana; or discover the Caribbean-Creole influences in Little Haiti. However, a word of warning: after dark, the downtown business district is not recommended for wandering tourists; nor is Little Haiti.

Greater Miami Convention & Visitors Bureau *701 Brickell Ave, Suite 2700,*

Miami

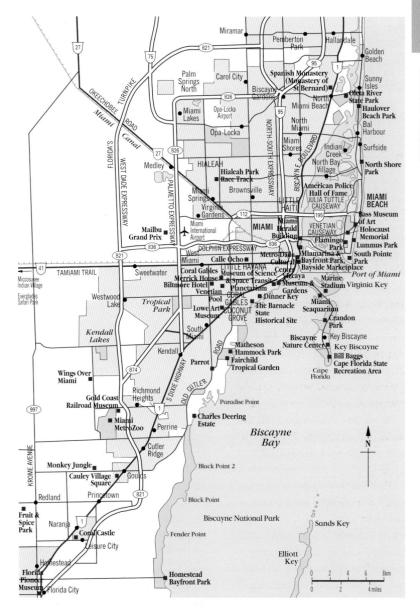

An Art Deco building

Miami, FL 33131. Tel: (305) 539 3000;
www.miamiandbeaches.com

Art Deco District

The world's largest collection of Art
Deco architecture, comprising some
800 individual buildings within a
2.5sq km (1sq mile) area on Miami
Beach. Ocean Drive is the centre of the
action – a favourite backdrop for
photographic fashion shoots, café
society and evening strolls past
spectacular neon-lit hotel façades
(*see pp30–31*).
Maps, information and guided walking
tours from the **Art Deco Welcome**
Center*, 1001 Ocean Drive, Miami Beach.*
Tel: (305) 672 2014; www.mdpl.org.
Open: Mon–Fri 11am–6pm, Sat
10am–10pm, Sun 11am–10pm.

Bass Museum of Art

A first-class permanent collection
of Old Master paintings, sculpture,
furniture and decorative arts is
augmented by a wide-ranging
calendar of special exhibitions.
2121 Park Ave, Miami Beach.
Tel: (305) 673 7530;
www.bassmuseum.org. Open: Tue–Sat
10am–5pm, Sun 11am–5pm.
Admission charge.

Bayfront Park

A 13ha (32 acre) open space
on the Biscayne bayfront offering
magnificent views of the cruise ships,
a concert amphitheatre, jogging paths
and several memorials, including the
John F Kennedy Memorial Torch of
Friendship – symbolising Miami's ties
with Latin America. There's also the
Miami Skylift, a passenger-carrying
helium balloon that allows a bird's-eye
view over the city.

WATER TAXIS

Miami's water-taxi service is a great way
to get around the downtown area and
Miami Beach.

The downtown shuttle stops off at such
key hotel, shopping and dining locations as
the Biscayne Marriott, the Port of Miami,
Bayside Marketplace, the Sheraton Biscayne,
Brickell Key and the Hyatt Regency.

The Miami Beach Marina stop is
convenient for Ocean Drive; and there is also
a stop for the trendy Lincoln Road Mall
shopping district.

Services operate daily from noon.
Tel: toll free (954) 467 6677.

*101 Biscayne Blvd, Downtown
(adjacent to Bayside Marketplace);
www.bayfrontparkmiami.com.
Skylift Sun–Thur 10am–7pm, Fri & Sat
10am–10pm. Admission charge.*

Bayside Marketplace

This lively shopping, entertainment and
dining complex overlooks the yachts
moored in Miamarina. Browse around
the 150 or so stores and the craft
market, sample international cuisine,
enjoy the antics of street performers,
and tune in to the daily concerts.
Bayside is accessible from the Port of
Miami by water-taxi service which
serves the downtown area and Miami
Beach (*see box*).
*401 North Biscayne Blvd.
Tel: (305) 577 3344;
www.baysidemarketplace.com.
Open: Mon–Thur 10am–10pm, Fri & Sat
10am–11pm, Sun 11am–9pm; extended
hours at restaurants, bars & cafés.*

Bill Baggs Cape Florida State Recreation Area

This natural preserve at the tip of Key
Biscayne has been planted with native
South Florida trees and its 1.6km
(1 mile) long sandy beach is one of the
best spots on the bayfront. You'll find
snack bars and barbecue areas plus
bicycles, snorkelling gear and fishing
tackle for hire.
*1200 South Crandon Blvd, Key Biscayne.
Tel: (305) 361 5811;
www.floridastateparks.org. Open: daily
8am–sunset. Admission charge.*

Brigade 2506 Memorial

The eternal flame of this memorial
commemorates counter-revolutionaries
who landed near Cuba's Bay of Pigs in
an unsuccessful attempt to overthrow
Fidel Castro in 1961.
*SW 8th St & SW 13th Ave (Little
Havana). Free admission.*

Coral Castle

A 20-year labour of love, this truly
bizarre 1,100 ton carved coral rock
edifice was built single-handedly by
lovesick Latvian Edward Leedskalnin,
and is said to be a memorial to the
sweetheart who jilted him. It includes
coral rock furniture, solar-heated bath
tubs and a 9 ton gate.
*28655 South Dixie Hwy, Homestead.
Tel: (305) 248 6345;
www.coralcastle.com. Open: Sun–Thur
8am–6pm, Fri & Sat 8am–9pm.
Admission charge.*

Tropical and subtropical plants surround
George Merrick's former home

Coral Gables Merrick House

The Merrick family home takes its name from its Spanish-style roof tiles made from local coral. Coral Gables' founder, George Merrick, spent his teens here, and many of the furnishings and artefacts are genuine family pieces. The pretty gardens have been planted with a variety of native shrubs, scented jasmine and fruit trees.

907 Coral Way, Coral Gables.
Tel: (305) 460 5361. Open: guided
tours Wed & Sun 1pm, 2pm & 3pm;
gardens daily until sunset.
Admission charge.

The famous pink flamingoes at Jungle Island

Everglades Safari Park

Experience Florida's exotic 'river of grass' by airboat. You can also explore the jungle trails by foot, watch alligator wrestling performed and tour a replica of a Chickee Village.

26700 Tamiami Trail, Miami.
Tel: (305) 226 6923;
www.evsafaripark.com. Open: daily
9am–5pm. Admission charge.

Fairchild Tropical Garden

These botanical gardens are claimed to be the largest in the continental USA, including 34ha (83 acres) of tropical plants, rolling lawns and clear lakes. Narrated tram tours give an overview of the grounds, and visitors are invited to explore special rainforest, mangrove and Everglades areas, as well as the rare plant house.

10901 Old Cutler Rd, Coral Gables.
Tel: (305) 667 1651;

www.fairchildgarden.org. Open: daily
9.30am–5pm. Admission charge.

Fruit and Spice Park

There is a distinctly international flavour to this exotic 8ha (20 acre) site. More than 500 varieties of fruits, nuts, spices and herbs are cultivated here, many of them on sale in the gift shop.

24801 SW 187th Ave, Homestead.
Tel: (305) 247 5727;
www.fruitandspicepark.org.
Open: daily 10am–5pm.
Admission charge.

Gold Coast Railroad Museum

This collection of historic locomotives, rolling stock (including a presidential Pullman car used by presidents Roosevelt, Truman, Eisenhower, Reagan and George Bush Snr), and

railroad memorabilia is just the ticket for train buffs. Train rides are a weekend highlight.
12450 SW 152nd St, Kendall. Tel: (305) 253 0063; www.goldcoast-railroad.org. Open: Mon–Fri 10am–4pm, Sat & Sun 11am–4pm. Admission charge.

Haulover Beach Park
A 1.5km (1 mile) stretch of natural dunes and seashore offering excellent facilities, including picnic areas, a children's playground, boat hire, family golf course, walking trails and tennis courts.
10800 Collins Ave, North Miami Beach. Tel: (305) 947 3525; www.miamidade.gov. Open: daily sunrise–sunset. Free admission.

Jungle Island
Jungle Island's brightly coloured cast of more than 1,000 exotic birds is complemented by orangutans, snakes and crocodiles, all of whom take part in regular shows throughout the day; you can also feed the famous pink flamingoes.
1111 Parrot Jungle Trail, Watson Island. Tel: (305) 400 7000; www.jungleisland.com. Open: daily 10am–6pm. Admission charge.

Lowe Art Museum
The exceptional Kress Collection of Renaissance and Baroque art is the highlight of this elegant small museum. It also features Spanish masterpieces, 19th- to 20th-century American works, Chinese porcelain, plus Asian, South American and Native American artefacts among its treasures.
1301 Stanford Drive, Coral Gables. Tel: (305) 284 3535; www.lowemuseum.org. Open: Tue, Wed, Fri & Sat 10am–5pm, Thur noon–7pm, Sun noon–5pm. Admission charge.

Metro-Dade Cultural Center
A landmark cultural centre which houses a trio of municipal showcases: the **Miami Art Museum** of Dade County, which focuses on Western art post-1945; the state-of-the-art **County Library**; and the admirable **Historical Museum** of Southern Florida. At the latter, life-sized dioramas depict 10,000 years of local history with the help of artefacts and hands-on displays.
101 West Flagler St, Downtown. Art Museum. Tel: (305) 375 1700; www.miamiartmuseum.org. Historical Museum. Tel: (305) 375 1492; www.hmsf.org. Open: Mon–Sat (except Art Museum, closed Mon) 10am–5pm (every third Thur until 9pm), Sun noon–5pm. Admission charge.

Miami Children's Museum
A thoughtful family alternative to the theme parks, with two floors of interactive exhibits, from a climbable two-storey sandcastle to a TV studio and a climbing wall.
980 MacArthur Causeway, Watson Island. Tel: (305) 375 5437; www.miamichildrensmuseum.org. Open: daily 10am–6pm. Admission charge.

Architectural extravaganzas

Enthusiastic developers have long believed that anything is possible in Miami. Architects inspired by the vision of wide blue skies, exotic palm trees and balmy temperatures have been positively encouraged to let their imagination run riot. A happy result of this is that in addition to the famous Art Deco District (*see p22*), Miami is home to many other splendid and bizarre examples of 20th-century architecture.

Take, for instance, James Deering's Vizcaya (*see p29*). A short drive from the sheer glass and steel monuments to high finance of Brickell Avenue, this lavish 70-room Italianate villa, completed in 1918, is one of the earliest examples of the Miami construction boom.

Spanish-Mediterranean was the preferred style for Coral Gables, George Merrick's 'City Beautiful', founded in 1921. Among the special features here is the grand Puerto del Sol entrance, the enchanting Venetian Pool (*see p29*) and Merrick's pet project, The Villages. These seven enclaves of distinctive vernacular architecture range in style from Chinese and Italian to French and early Florida. Unfortunately, an unnamed 1926 hurricane and the depression of the 1930s prevented Merrick from completing many of his projects. The 90m (300ft) Spanish tower atop the imposing 1925 Biltmore Hotel is a local landmark.

Another themed community was Glenn Curtiss' Opa-Locka, a 1926 Moorish-style development in North Miami. Drawing inspiration from *1,001 Tales from the Arabian Nights*, Curtiss' architect was instructed to lay out streets in the shape of a crescent moon, and to adorn buildings with all manner of Moorish domes, minarets and painted tiles.

The Italian-style Vizcaya

The towering Biltmore Hotel

On a more classical note, elegant Hialeah Park is one of the most beautiful horse-racing courses in the world, with its ivy-covered French-style clubhouse, completed in 1932. The eye-catching blue-and-white tiled façade of the Bacardi Imports Building (*2100 Biscayne Boulevard*) also dates from the 1930s, while further south on the same street, the Freedom Tower strikes a surprise Old-World note on the Downtown skyline. It was built in 1925 for the *Miami News* as a copy of the Giralda Tower in Seville, Spain. Later, it was used to process Cuban refugees, hence the name.

The 1950s stamped their own style on Miami with such extravaganzas as the Fountainbleau Hotel. By this time, the small Art Deco hotels were considered passé and architects such as Morris Lapidus built hotels that affirmed the American spirit of the 1950s that bigger was better. Even if you are not a guest, take time to wander through the lobby and spectacular pool just to feel the energy created by the army of bellhops, concierges and travellers.

The late decades of the 20th century saw skyscrapers swallow up much of the remaining land, but the waterfront has been preserved with plentiful parkspace and people places such as Bayfront Park, with its gentle meandering curves. Who knows what new styles will hallmark this millennium?

Miami Metro Zoo

This is one of the largest 'cageless' zoos in the USA. Natural habitats have been created to simulate the African veldt and jungle forests, and a 3km (2 mile) monorail circuit ensures a bird's-eye view of the residents. Highlights include a giraffe feeding station, a rare white Bengal tiger and a range of appealing animal shows.

12400 SW 152nd St, South Miami.
Tel: (305) 251 0400;
www.miamimetrozoo.com. Open: daily
9.30am–5.30pm. Admission charge.

Miami Museum of Science and Space Transit Planetarium

A gripping voyage of exploration through the mysteries of science and space enlivened by more than 140 hands-on displays, multimedia shows, robotic dinosaurs, virtual reality basketball and a planetarium. Natural history exhibits include an outdoor Wildlife Center which rehabilitates injured birds.

3280 South Miami Ave, Coconut Grove.
Tel: (305) 646 4200; www.miamisci.org.
Open: daily 10am–6pm.
Admission charge.

Miami Seaquarium

A fun outing for all the family, the Seaquarium offers an educational look at the marine world with exciting shows. Check out the manatees, dip into the touch tanks, watch the shark-feeding and take your seats for Lolita the killer whale, TV star Flipper the dolphin, and the comical Salty the Sea Lion show.

4400 Rickenbacker Causeway.
Tel: (305) 361 5705;
www.miamiseaquarium.com.
Open: daily 9.30am; closing times vary
by season. Admission charge.

Miccosukee Indian Village and Airboat Tours

This is a chance for visitors to catch a glimpse of the 'traditional' Miccosukee Indian way of life – now sadly commercialised to something of a sideshow. Demonstrations of native crafts and alligator wrestling take place, and there is a museum, as well as a restaurant serving Miccosukee-inspired food. You can also explore the Everglades by airboat.

Mile Marker 70, Tamiami Trail, 20km
(30 miles) west of downtown on US41.
Tel: (305) 552 8365;
www.miccosukeetribe.com. Open: daily
9am–5pm. Admission charge.

Monkey Jungle

In 1933, animal behaviourist Joe Dumond released six macaque monkeys in a 4ha (10 acre) hardwood hammock (small wood) intending to study their habits. However, running short of funds he caged in walkways for visitors and the free-ranging macaque colony developed into a popular attraction. Now, around 500 primates (mostly running free) represent 30 species of monkeys, and you can watch them dive into a pool to get fruit at feeding times.

14805 SW 216th St, Homestead.
Tel: (305) 235 1611;

In 1926, the Venetian Pool was drained to host a performance by the Miami Opera

www.monkeyjungle.com. Open: daily 9.30am–5pm. Admission charge.

Spanish Monastery

Strange but true: Miami is the unlikely site of the oldest building in the USA. Newspaper magnate William Randolph Hearst bought the 12th-century cloisters of St Bernard's Monastery and shipped them from Segovia, Spain, in 1929. Re-erected in 1954, they now serve as an Episcopal church.
16711 West Dixie Hwy, North Miami Beach. Tel: (305) 945 1461; www.spanishmonastery.com. Open: guided tours Mon–Sat 9am–4.30pm, Sun noon–4.30pm. Admission charge.

Venetian Pool

This Venetian-inspired lagoon, complete with little humpbacked bridges, grottoes and waterfalls (all carved out of an old coral rock quarry), is one of the most unusual and delightful swimming pools imaginable. In its heyday, the Miami Opera, Tarzan star Johnny Weissmuller and bathing belle Esther Williams all performed here. Now visitors can bask on the sandy beach, bathe in the crystal-clear water fed by a natural spring, and find refreshments in the courtyard café.
2701 De Soto Blvd, Coral Gables. Tel: (305) 460 5306; www.venetianpool.com. Open: Tue–Fri 11am–5.30pm (till 7.30pm in July), Sat & Sun 10am–4.30pm. Admission charge.

Vizcaya Museum and Gardens

Built between 1916 and 1918 as a winter home for industrialist James Deering, this palatial Italian Renaissance-style villa is one of Miami's finest attractions. It is set back from Biscayne Bay in 4ha (10 acres) of formal landscaped gardens, and acts as a showcase for Deering's treasure trove of 15th- to 19th-century antiques. Each of the 34 rooms is devoted to a different style and period, including a Renaissance Hall, a classical 18th-century English Adam-style Library and a magnificent Rococo Salon.
3251 South Miami Ave, Coconut Grove. Tel: (305) 250 9133; www.vizcayamuseum.org. Open: daily 9.30am–4.30pm. Admission charge.

Walk: Art Deco District

In 1915, John Collins borrowed $50,000 and began to develop Miami Beach. As the mangrove wilderness was cleared, the first homes and hotels appeared, many built in the popular 1920s Mediterranean Revival-style. In the 1930s and 1940s, Miami Beach emerged as a showcase for the dashing new Art Deco architects. Rescued from decay in the 1970s, today's rejuvenated Art Deco District is one of the world's most fashionable places.

Allow 3 hours.

Start on Ocean Drive at 6th St. Stroll up to the Art Deco Welcome Center.

1 Ocean Drive

Facing the ocean across Lummus Park and the beach, Ocean Drive unfurls in a magnificent sweep of Art Deco delights: streamlined façades, bold vertical planes, racing stripes, 'eyebrow' windows and nautical and geometric motifs. The Park Central (*No 630*) employs all manner of these deco devices. Also note the name-sake neon-lit tower atop the Waldorf (*No 860*) and ship's prow on the Breakwater (*No 940*), which shares a pool with the Mediterranean-Revival Edison (*No 960*).

Stop at the Welcome Center (see p22) for information and maps, then head away from the beach on 10th St.

2 10th Street

A short walk down 10th Street leads to the Essex Hotel, with an etched glass flamingo on the porch door. Opposite,

the Fairwind Hotel boasts extravagant neon. The huge Washington Storage Building (*1001 Washington Ave*), with

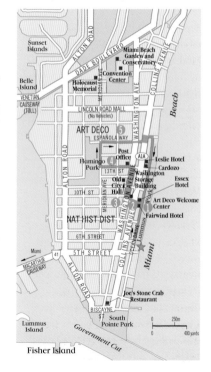

its window grilles and Spanish Baroque-style carved reliefs, is now home to the **Wolfsonian Foundation**, which exhibits decorative and propaganda arts.

Tel: (305) 531 1001. Open: Mon, Tue, Sat & Sun noon–6pm, Thur & Fri noon–9pm. Admission charge.
Turn right on to Washington Ave.

3 Washington Avenue

Just north on Washington Avenue there is a clutch of modest 1930s hotels: the Park Washington, Taft and Kenmore (*Nos 1020, 1044 & 1050*), now all part of the Best Western chain. The 1927 Old City Hall (*No 1130*) is a nine-storey Mediterranean affair decorated with giant urns. Take a moment to visit the Depression Moderne-style Post Office (*No 1300*). Its rotunda has a mural and painted ceiling above the semicircle of original brass mail boxes.

Walk west (left) on 13th St.

4 Apartment buildings

On 13th Street, pretty Chrisken Court (*No 541*) features hefty wooden balconies and decorative reliefs. The Parkway Apartments, on the corner of Meridian Avenue, enjoy a balconied courtyard, colourful tiled steps and niches filled with urns. The upper section of Spanish-themed, gas-lit Española Way has several restored apartment houses such as the simple Streamlined Allen (*No 609–611*) and Mediterranean (*No 531–525*).

Walk north (right) on Meridian Ave, and return east (right) on Española Way.

5 Española Way

From Drexel Avenue, William Whitman's 1922 Spanish Village runs for a block east on Española Way. The tree-shaded sidewalks are lined with cafés, boutiques, jewellers and retro dealers selling second-hand clothes and antiques beneath a cheerful array of striped awnings and balconies. Take a break here before returning to the top end of Ocean Drive.

Cross Washington Ave, opposite the Cameo Cinema (a model of 3 ton Streamlined Vitralite). On the corner of Collins Ave, turn left by the former Hoffman's Caféteria (No 1450), with its distinctive cut-out corner façade. Take the first right and rejoin Ocean Drive.

Palm trees and candy-striped awnings shade shoppers on Española Way

Tour: Coconut Grove and Coral Gables

Coconut Grove is one of Miami's oldest and most attractive neighbourhoods. It is a good place to begin this 16km (10 mile) jaunt, which includes a detour around Coral Gables, the Fairchild Tropical Garden and a swimming opportunity.

Make it a day trip and pack a picnic.

From Grand Ave, opposite Cocowalk, take Main Highway south.

1 Coconut Grove

There were only two coconut palms in the 'grove' when Horace P Porter opened his Post Office in 1873. Early visitors to the area stayed in rustic cabins along the shore. Today, the sidewalks may be brick and the streetlamps Victorian, but the Grove is hip and happening. Great shopping and good restaurants abound. On the corner of Charles Avenue, where 19th-century Bahamanian immigrants built traditional wood-frame 'conch' homes, is the Spanish Rococo-style Coconut Grove Playhouse.
Take Main Highway south.

2 The Barnacle

A suitable name for a home designed by a naval architect. Ralph Middleton Munroe built this fine two-storey house in 1891. The inspired period furnishings include paintings and photographs.

3485 Main Highway, Coconut Grove.
Tel: (305) 448 9445;
www.floridastateparks.org/thebarnacle.
Open: guided tours Fri–Mon 10am, 11.30am, 1pm & 2.30pm.
Admission charge.
Continue on Main Highway.

3 Plymouth Congregational Church

This weathered stone church was designed in the style of a Spanish mission building. Its 400-year-old oak and walnut door came from the Pyrenees, and there is a quiet garden cloister around to the right.
Turn right on Poinciana Ave, cross Le Jeune Rd for Miller Rd and the intersection with Maggiore St.

4, 5 and 6 Coral Gables villages

A special feature of George Merrick's 'City Beautiful', these small groups of houses are not villages in the real sense, and some only cover a single block. The tiny Chinese Village (4) features sweeping roofs in green, yellow and blue, cut-out oriental motifs and bamboo-design window grilles. South on Hardee Road, the French Country Village (5) employs towers, pointed slate 'witches-hat' roofs and wooden shutters. Further south on San Vicente Street, the pretty, whitewashed Dutch Colonial Village (6) is particularly striking with its gables, red-tiled roofs and twisted barley sugar chimneys etched against a deep blue sky.

Go south on Le Jeune Rd to Cartagena Plaza, then south on Old Cutler Rd.

7 Matheson Hammock Country Park

A terrific bayside park with a beach, picnic tables, refreshments, walking trails and bike paths among the mangroves.
9610 Old Cutler Rd, Coral Gables. Tel: (305) 665 5475. Open: daily 8am–sunset. Admission charge for cars. Continue south on Old Cutler Rd.

8 Fairchild Tropical Garden

Beautiful tropical gardens (*see p24*).
Return to Cartagena Plaza. Head north to the traffic lights on Le Jeune Rd, then right on to Ingraham Highway to rejoin Main Highway, and return to Coconut Grove.

Tour: Coconut Grove and Coral Gables

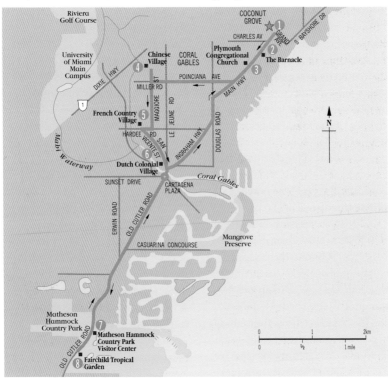

Fort Lauderdale

An hour's journey north of Miami, Fort Lauderdale is one of Florida's leading beach resorts, and its five-star cruise facility, Port Everglades, serves over 2½ million cruise passengers each year. Fort Lauderdale is all glitter, from the tips of its Downtown skyscrapers to the maze of sparkly waterways that have earned it the nickname the 'Venice of America'. It is a brash but friendly Gold Coast success story and is one of the fastest growing cities in the state.

The first settlers

The city is named after Major William Lauderdale, who established the first of three small forts here in the 1830s. In 1893, pioneer settler Frank Stranahan established an overnight camp for the Bay Biscayne Stagecoach Line, and traded provisions for alligator hides, pelts and egret plumes brought to him by the local Seminole Indians. With the arrival of the railroad in 1896, a small settlement grew around the trading post and attracted the attention of Florida State Governor Napoleon Bonaparte Broward, who unveiled a grand plan to drain the Everglades.

Dredging operations began along the New River in 1906. Then, during the 1920s land boom, a Venetian land-building technique, known as 'finger-islanding', was used to transform the mangrove swamps between the river and the Intracoastal Waterway into a network of channels and building plots. Today, the city's 200km (300 miles) of navigable inland waterways are one of its top attractions, plied by sightseeing boats, private yachts and a handy water-taxi service.

Golden opportunities

From the 1950s through to the 1970s, Fort Lauderdale was infamous for its raucous spring break student parties. However, following a clampdown by the authorities, the students have moved on and the city has emerged as a popular year-round family tourist destination.

Together with its neighbouring beachside communities, Greater Fort Lauderdale offers 37km (23 miles) of golden beaches, historic homes, modern museums, fine shopping and a range of family attractions. Top-class facilities, such as the magnificent Broward Center for the Performing Arts, complement the city's dynamic cultural programme.

For outdoor types, there are sporting opportunities galore, from golf, diving, sailing and sport fishing to tennis.

Fort Lauderdale

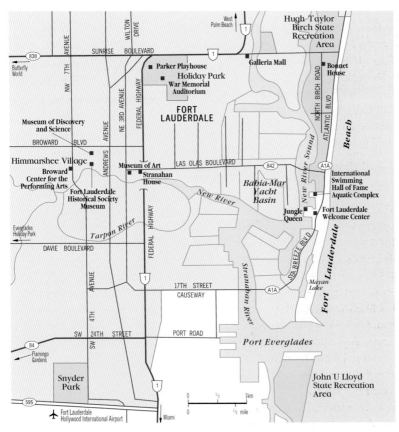

Spectators can enjoy such fast and furious sports as *jai-alai* (a version of the Basque *pelota*, involving a small ball being hurled at speeds of up to 280kph/175mph with the aid of curved wicker slings attached to players' hands) at Dania, horse-racing at Gulfstream Park and weekly rodeos in Davie.

Bonnet House

This lovely plantation-style house is set in a leafy 15ha (35 acre) estate, just a stone's throw from the Downtown skyscrapers. Artists Frederick Clay Bartlett and his wife, Evelyn, designed the eclectic and unusual interior with a rich collection of decorative and fine arts. Namesake bonnet lilies grow around a miniature lake in the grounds.
900 N Birch Rd. Tel: (954) 563 5393; www.bonnethouse.org. Open: guided tours only, Tue–Sat 10am–4pm, Sun noon–4pm. Closed Mon. Admission charge.

Butterfly World

This popular attraction provides a dazzling insight into the insect world. Around 150 species of butterflies inhabit huge walk-through aviaries, planted with tropical foliage. There's also an insectarium, a museum and the USA's largest free-flight hummingbird aviary. *Tradewinds Park South, 3600 W Sample Rd, Coconut Creek.*

Tel: (954) 977 4400; www.butterflyworld.com. Open: Mon–Sat 9am–5pm, Sun 11am–5pm. Admission charge.

Everglades Holiday Park Airboat Tours

Skim across the shallow marshes on an airboat for a real Everglades experience, which includes a visit to a

The courtyard of Bonnet House

replica Seminole Indian village and views of Southern Florida's unique flora and fauna.

21940 Griffin Rd. Tel: (954) 434 8111; www.evergladesholidaypark.com. Open: daily tours every 30 minutes from 9am–5pm. Admission charge.

Flamingo Gardens

One of the area's earliest citrus groves has been transformed into a splendid garden bursting with exotic blooms and towering trees inhabited by a collection of animals and birds including monkeys, crocodiles, alligators and, of course, flamingoes.

A tram ride explores the 24ha (60 acre) site, which also boasts a bird of prey centre, museum and store.

*3750 Flamingo Rd, Davie.
Tel: (954) 473 2955;
www.flamingogardens.org.*

TROLLEY TOURS AND WATER TAXIS

Here are two great ways to get around Fort Lauderdale and see the sights: **South Florida Trolley Tours** offer daily narrated historical tours in old San Francisco-style trams with pick-ups from all major hotels (*tel: (954) 492 3100 for information*).

Fort Lauderdale's **water taxis** navigate the Intracoastal Waterway and New River with stops at a variety of waterside locations from shopping centres to restaurants and attractions. The service operates daily from 10am, and the set fare allows unlimited rides all day.

Pick up a taxi from the dock in the port, or call the operator (*tel: (954) 467 6677*) and make a booking.

Open: daily 9.30–5.30pm. Closed: Mon 1 June–30 Sept. Admission charge.

Hugh Taylor Birch State Recreation Area

A 73ha (180 acre) green breathing space, locked between the beachfront and Intracoastal Waterway. Walk or cycle around the 3km (2 mile) circuit, investigate the short beach hardwood hammock trail, or rent a canoe and look out for racoons, marsh rabbits and wading birds. A short film show at the visitor centre gives a potted history and introduction to the park.

3109 E Sunrise Blvd. Tel: (954) 564 4521; www.floridastateparks.org/ hughtaylorbirch. Open: daily 8am–dusk. Admission charge.

International Swimming Hall of Fame Aquatic Complex

The Hall of Fame features a terrific array of swimming memorabilia in its museum wing. There are displays on all-time greats such as Johnny 'Tarzan' Weissmuller and Mark Spitz, plus Olympic gold medals, swimwear through the ages and much more. The Aquatic Complex, with its two Olympic pools and diving facilities, is patronised by Olympic hopefuls and it is also open to the public.

501 Seabreeze Blvd. Tel: (954) 828 4580; www.ishof.org; http://ci.ftlaud.fl.us/flac. Open: Hall of Fame daily 9am–5pm; Aquatic Complex Mon–Fri 8am–4pm & 6–7.30pm, Sat & Sun 8am–2pm. Admission charge.

Las Olas Boulevard is a shopper's paradise

Jungle Queen

This old-style riverboat offers daily sightseeing cruises around the waterways of the 'Venice of America'. It glides past exclusive waterfront homes and stops off at a purpose-built Indian Village for a spot of alligator wrestling and souvenir shopping. At night, sail up the New River for a 'Bar-B-Que Ribs, Chicken & Shrimp Dinner Cruise' on a private island, an all-you-can-eat spread with entertainment in the form of a vaudeville show and an old-fashioned singalong.

Bahia Mar Yacht Center (off A1A), Fort Lauderdale Beach. Tel: (954) 462 5596 for schedules and information; www.junglequeen.com

Las Olas Boulevard

Fort Lauderdale's prettiest shopping street is a must on any holiday-maker's itinerary. Landscaped with flowers and trees, the boulevard is studded with a host of chic designer boutiques, art and antiques galleries and attractive restaurants.

Museum of Art

This state-of-the-art showcase is renowned for its fine collections of 19th- and 20th-century American and European paintings and sculpture. In addition, there are collections of ethnic art, and the gallery stages some interesting temporary exhibitions, as well as hosting an Artist in Residence programme. Drop in at the excellent museum store, too.
1 E Las Olas Blvd, Downtown.
Tel: (954) 525 5500; www.moafl.org.
Open: Fri–Wed 11am–7pm, Thur
11am–9pm. Admission charge.

Museum of Discovery and Science

A $30-million 'hands-on' museum packed with marvellous gadgets, games and educational exhibits which make learning lots of fun. There are seven display areas, ranging from the high-tech Runways to Rockets to the grassroots Florida EcoScapes with its walk-through guide to local habitats. Programme a robot, take a space ride on the Meteor Storm, or goggle in amazement at the five-storey-high IMAX cinema screen.
401 SW 2nd St. Tel: (954) 467 6637;
www.mods.org. Open: Mon–Sat
10am–5pm, Sun noon–6pm.
Admission charge.

Riverwalk

The landscaped Riverwalk was part of the city's massive urban redesign programme for the 1990s and provides access to Fort Lauderdale's prime river frontage. Stroll along the New River from Stranahan House up to the historic Himmarshee Village area and Broward Center for the Performing Arts, stopping off to admire the views from an outdoor café, picnic table or park bench.

Stranahan House

The oldest house in Broward County, this homely pioneer property was founded on the banks of the New River in 1900. Trader Frank Stranahan and his schoolteacher wife, Ivy Cromatie, lived here, and entertained East Coast railway baron Henry Flagler in the pine panelled living room. The interior has been restored in the style of 1913–15, with antique Victorian furniture and period pieces, together with photographs of Fort Lauderdale's early days.
335 E Las Olas Blvd (at SE 6th Ave).
Tel: (954) 524 4736;
www.stranahanhouse.com.
Open: guided tours only Wed–Sun 1pm,
1.30pm, 2pm, 2.30pm, 3pm, 3.30pm.
Admission charge.

The Everglades

The Native Americans called it *pa-hay-okee* or 'grassy waters', a name later paraphrased by ecologist Marjorie Stoneman Douglas as the title of her evocative book *The Everglades: River of Grass*. It is an accurate description of this vast waterlogged region which stretches from Lake Okeechobee in the north down to Florida Bay and the Gulf of Mexico. The endless vista of rippling, razor-sharp sawgrass was once a hideout for Seminole Indians who travelled the maze of secret waterways. Now it is the last refuge of the rare Florida panther and a haven for other endangered species such as the Everglades mink, American crocodile, roseate spoonbill, bald eagle and osprey.

The best time to visit the Everglades is during the dry winter season. Wildlife spotting is easier as the animals and birds gather around the deepwater sloughs (waterholes) to feed, and there are fewer mosquitoes to trouble you (but don't leave off the repellent even in winter). Over 2,000 plant species flourish in the

The Everglades are home to the American crocodile

subtropical conditions, and 45 of these are unique to the region. Rising above the marshy grasslands, shady hammocks (small woods) of willow, pine and tropical hardwoods such as mahogany and live oak cling to limestone outcrops, providing shelter for wildlife and a host for airplants, orchids and bromeliads. A less welcome guest is the parasitic strangler fig, dropping its tangled aerial roots to the ground and gradually depriving the host tree of water and light until it dies. Stands of elegant cypress trees are mirrored in the tannin-rich waters of quiet swamps.

The Everglades is itself endangered. Starting in the 1930s, a giant flood control system began diverting water to canals running to the gulf and the ocean. The unfortunate side effect of flood control has been a devastation of the wilderness. Birds have diminished, the black bear has been eliminated and the Florida panther is nearing extinction.

Serious steps are being taken to help both the cities and the Everglades live in harmony with each other. In 1947 Everglades National Park was created to preserve the slow moving 'river of grass'. In 1968 Biscayne National Park was established to protect the fragile coral reefs. And in 1974 Big Cypress National Preserve was

Everglades National Park is one of the world's most outstanding natural habitats.

established by an act of Congress to protect the watershed of Everglades National Park.

More than a score of government agencies and private conservation groups, in concert with industry, are working feverishly to secure the future of the Everglades. The next decade will determine its success or failure but for more information and updates, visit the Everglades Restoration Plan website, *www.evergladesplan.org*

Key West

The southernmost city in the USA, Key West is a popular stop with several cruise lines operating in the Caribbean. Measuring just 6.5km by 3km (4 miles by 2 miles), Key West remains at heart a village (albeit a rather exotic one). It is a quirky mix of old and new. Once the haunt of pirates and wreckers (more politely known as ship's salvagers), it is now a popular gay enclave and welcomes the annual winter invasion of tourists with amused tolerance.

While walking is the best way to savour the charms and relaxed atmosphere of Old Key West (the central nub of town), you can also be ferried around the main island sights aboard the Old Town Trolley, or take a 90-minute narrated tour on the Conch Train. Should you be ashore at dusk, the sunset celebrations on Mallory Dock, performed by a host of wacky street entertainers and musicians, are a near-legendary institution.

Audubon House and Gardens

The famous naturalist and artist John James Audubon never actually stayed in this fine 1830 house. However, he worked on his paintings in the garden while visiting the island in 1832 to study the native birds, and many of the works are displayed inside.
205 Whitehead St. Tel: (305) 294 2116; www.audubonhouse.com. Open: daily 9.30am–5pm. Admission charge.

Fort Zachary Taylor State Historic Site

Founded in 1845, Fort Zachary Taylor was a rare Union outpost in the south during the Civil War. Rescued from obscurity, it now houses a small museum and a large collection of Civil War cannons. On the shore, there is a public beach with picnic tables in the shade and a restaurant offering kayak rentals.
Southard St, in the Truman Annex. Tel: (305) 292 6713. Open: daily 8am–dusk. Admission charge.

Hemingway House

Ernest Hemingway moved into this mid-19th-century house in 1931 with his second wife, Pauline, and they furnished it with a mixture of Spanish, Cuban and African mementoes from their travels. The author wrote most of his finest work here, and his eight-toed cats' descendants still have the run of the place. The guided tours impart a wealth of anecdotal information.

907 Whitehead St. Tel: (305) 294 1136;
www.hemingwayhome.com.
Open: daily 9am–5pm. Admission charge.

Key West Aquarium

A local attraction since 1934, offering
aquariums, touch tanks, turtle pens
and shark-feeding opportunities for
fearless visitors.
1 Whitehead St. Tel: 1 800 868 7482;
www.keywestaquarium.com.
Open: daily 10am–6pm.
Admission charge.

Key West Lighthouse Museum

This 1848 lighthouse affords splendid
views over Key West and the coast
from its viewing balcony, reached by
way of 88 steps. There is an
interesting small museum in the
former Keeper's Quarters.
938 Whitehead St. Tel: (305) 294 0012;
www.kwahs.com. Open: daily 9.30am–
4.30pm. Admission charge.

Little White House Museum

President Harry S Truman's 'alternative
White House' during his six years in
office, this late 19th-century house has
been restored in the style of the 1940s.
111 Front St, Truman Annex.
Tel: (305) 294 9911;
www.trumanlittlewhitehouse.com.
Open: daily 9am–5pm. Admission charge.

Mel Fisher Maritime Heritage Museum

Gold bullion, jewellery, silver
tableware, and other treasures salvaged
from Spanish wrecks by Key West's
most famous treasure hunter, Mel
Fisher, are on display here. Start
with the riveting video presentation
and end at the shop where souvenirs
are on sale.
200 Greene St. Tel: (305) 294 2633;
www.melfisher.org. Open: daily
9.30am–5pm. Admission charge.

Wrecker's Museum

Key West's oldest house, this 1829 sea
captain's home evokes a distinctly
nautical air. It contains period
furnishings and all manner of artefacts,
model ships, pictures and documents
relating to the 19th-century wrecking
(that is, salvage) industry.
322 Duval St. Tel: (305) 294 9502.
Open: Thur–Sat 10am–2pm.
Admission charge.

The lighthouse is now a museum and can be
visited

Antigua

The largest of the Leeward Islands, Antigua (pronounced An-tee-ga) combines some of the Caribbean's finest white sand beaches with several interesting historical sites. The island was sighted by Christopher Columbus on his second voyage to the New World in 1493, and named after Santa Maria de la Antigua, a miraculous statue of the Virgin in Seville Cathedral.

Its earliest inhabitants were Stone Age Ciboney people who migrated from South America around 4,000 years ago. The Ciboneys, and their successors, the Arawaks, left their mark on several Amerindian sites, especially around Indian Town. An English colony from St Kitt's established the first permanent European settlement here in 1632 and, except for two brief periods of occupation by the French and Spanish, Antigua remained linked to Britain until full independence in 1981.

Antigua's scalloped, irregular coastline is one of its chief delights. They say there are 365 beaches – one for every day of the year. Fine natural harbours such as St John's, Falmouth and English Harbour have welcomed sailors for generations, and sailing is big news on the island.

The Caribbean's winter sailing calendar culminates in April/May with Antigua Race Week, a major international regatta and week-long celebration.

Looking out over English Harbour from Shirley Heights, Antigua

Pillars from a former sail loft in the garden of the Admiral's Inn, Nelson's Dockyard

Antigua Department of Tourism

Govt. Complex, Queen Elizabeth Hwy. PO Box 363, St John's. Tel: (268) 462 0480; www.antigua-barbuda.org. There is also a tourist information booth on the dock at Heritage Quay, St John's.

St John's

The entrance to St John's Harbour is guarded by Fort Barrington and Fort James, two of the numerous 18th-century defensive structures built by the British.

Behind the forts, the attractive West Indian town climbs gently back from the wharf in a friendly jumble of clapboard houses, fretwork balconies and roadside stalls to **St John's Cathedral**.

The impressive church building is flanked by its twin towers topped with silver cupolas. Erected in the mid-19th century on the site of two previous churches, the dignified wooden interior is worth a visit for its barrel ceilings supported by octagonal pillars, the decorative upper gallery, and grand memorials bedecked with coats of arms and purple prose.

Church Lane. Free admission.

Museum of Antigua and Barbuda

Housed in the Old Court House, built in 1750, this small museum traces the history of Antigua and its tiny sister island Barbuda. Relics of the ancient Ciboney and Arawak Indians include grinding stones, axe heads and conch shell chisels. There are sections on the plantation era, local flora and birdlife, but pride of place goes to the cricket bat of former West Indies and Antigua cricket captain Viv Richards.

Corner of Market & Long Sts. Tel: (268) 462 1469; www.antiguamuseums.org. Open: Mon–Thur 8.30am–3pm, Fri 8.30am–4pm, Sat 10am–2pm. Free admission.

Dark Wood Beach and Crab Hill

A Caribbean idyll – a crescent of soft, pale sand bordering clear, turquoise waters and fringed by palms – Dark Wood Beach is almost deserted during the week, but busy at the weekend. There are good beach bars here.

Further south, Johnson's Point is another quiet sand strip on Crab Hill Bay. Look out for the shell-lined steps to The Nature of Things, a fantastic shell shop in Crab Hill Village. The interior is a veritable treasury of conch shells and coral, sea urchins, starfish, barracuda heads sporting marbles for eyes, loofahs and sponges perched on shelves, balanced on beams, and cradled in fishing nets.

Dickinson Bay

Just north of St John's, Fort James Beach is the closest beach to the capital, but many short-stay visitors prefer to head a little further north to the resort area at Dickinson Bay. It provides silky sand, watersports including windsurfer and Hobie Cat (catamaran) hire, plus a welcome choice of beachside bars and restaurants in the shade.

English Harbour and Falmouth

One of the safest natural anchorages in the world, English Harbour was the British Admiralty's Caribbean base throughout the 18th and 19th centuries. Falmouth, nearby, was once the capital of Antigua, and the two bays, divided by a narrow isthmus fortified by the British, are now busy yachting anchorages during the winter season.

Horatio Nelson was posted to English Harbour in 1784. The young captain of HMS *Boreas*, a 28-gun frigate, was not amused. He considered Antigua a 'barbarous place', and fell out with the locals for enforcing the Navigation Act (banning trade with US vessels) too vigorously. Angry businessmen sued him for loss of earnings, and the future naval hero was

Naval Officers' House in Nelson's Dockyard, English Harbour

forced to spend eight weeks on board his ship to avoid imprisonment. John Herbert of the Montpelier Plantation, Nevis (*see p118*), put up Nelson's £10,000 bail, and when he went ashore to dine with his benefactor, Nelson met his wife-to-be, Fanny Nesbit. At the wedding, Fanny was given away by Nelson's friend Prince William Henry, later King William IV, who lived at **Clarence House** overlooking the harbour (*see p48*). Despite Nelson's aversion to the place, his name lingers on at **Nelson's Dockyard**, English Harbour's splendidly restored Georgian dockyard, which served as the British naval base in the Eastern Caribbean during the colonial era (*see pp48–9*). *South coast, via All Saints.*

Palm-fringed Dark Wood Beach on Antigua's southwest coast

The northeast

If you want to explore far from the madding crowd, there are several pleasant spots dotted around the central and northeastern corner of the island.

Betty's Hope

Betty's Hope was one of Antigua's chief 17th-century sugar plantations. Among the ruins, a stone windmill and its machinery have been restored and there is a small museum in the visitors' centre. *Off central island road to Indian Town. www.antiguamuseums.org. Open: Tues–Sat 10am–4pm. Admission charge.*

Harmony Hall

This fine old stone house, built around a sugar mill, is a perfect spot for shopping and lunch, and you can even take a dip in the swimming pool. This is principally an art gallery selling the work of local artists and high-quality Caribbean crafts. There is a breezy bar and lookout point in the old mill overlooking Nonsuch Bay. *East coast. Tel: (268) 460 4120; www.harmonyhallantigua.com. Open: daily 10am–6pm. Free admission.*

Indian Town National Park

It's a scenic drive across the east coast and Indian Town National Park, where the Atlantic surf has carved blowholes and an impressive arch, known as Devil's Bridge, out of the limestone cliffs. This is a spectacular place on a blustery day, with great views of the islands offshore. *Northeast coast.*

Parham

In the middle of the north coast, Parham, a small fishing village with an unusual octagonal church, is one of the oldest settlements on Antigua. *Central north coast.*

Tour: Exploring the southern coast

A great day out which takes in English Harbour, scenic Fig Tree Drive, and a chance to visit one of Antigua's most beautiful beaches, this tour can be accomplished either in a long morning, or at a more relaxing pace with a stop for lunch in Nelson's Dockyard.

Allow 4 to 6 hours.

Start at Shirley Heights.

1 Shirley Heights

Named after General Sir Thomas Shirley, Governor of the Leeward Islands between 1781 and 1791, the fortified hills above English Harbour afford a magnificent view over the sheltered bays and across to the island of Guadeloupe. Remains of the 18th-century signal station, which could give advance warning of a French attack, and the once sizeable military complex are scattered over a large area.
Drive down to Dow's Hill.

2 Dow's Hill Interpretation Centre

Start off in the modern Interpretation Centre with a 15-minute Sound and Light show depicting scenes from Antiguan history. The multimedia presentation traces the island's settlement by South American Indians, through the European Age of Discovery and Plantation era to the present day. Then step outside to enjoy views from the lookout point perched on the ruins of the Belvedere, the 18th-century governor's residence.
Tel: (268) 460 2777. Open: daily 9am–5pm. Admission charge.
Continue to Clarence House.

3 Clarence House

Off the road leading down from Shirley Heights to Nelson's Dockyard, Clarence House (*Open: 9am–5pm*) was built for Prince William Henry, Duke of Clarence (later William IV of England) in 1786. The house now serves as official summer home for the Governor General; when he's not in residence, the caretaker usually gives informal tours of the interior, with its period furnishings. In the past, distinguished guests have included Sir Winston Churchill and Princess Margaret.
Drive on to Nelson's Dockyard.

4 Nelson's Dockyard

Abandoned by the British Navy in 1889, this small Georgian dockyard was rescued from ruin in the 1960s and restored to its present spick-and-span state of grey-shuttered stone and wooden buildings.

Just inside the gates, a former pitch, tar and turpentine store has been transformed into the Admiral's Inn, a small hotel. The 16 massive pillars in its gardens once supported a sail loft: boats would berth in the narrow dock below while their sails were whipped up into an overhead loft for repair. At the **Nelson Museum** in the Admiral's House (*Tel: (268) 460 1379; www.antiguamuseums.com. Open: daily 8am–6pm. Admission charge*), period prints depict Nelson's man-of-war-style funeral carriage, and there is an old cookhouse which is now a bakery. An attractive brick building flanked by rounded cisterns used to store water, the

Admiral's Inn sleeps guests in rooms named after famous naval battles. The open-sided Working Mast House is still in use today, while the former 1821 Officers' Quarters now house galleries selling crafts, old maps and reproduction prints.

Continue northwards along the All Saints road. Shortly after Liberta, turn left for Sweets and Old Rd.

5 Fig Tree Drive

A rare corner of natural vegetation which escaped the 17th- and 18th-century sugar-cane boom. Lined with palms and banana plants, this lovely road is the most scenic on the island and winds down to the coast.

Head west (right) along the coast, past Dark Wood Beach (see p46), to visit St John's.

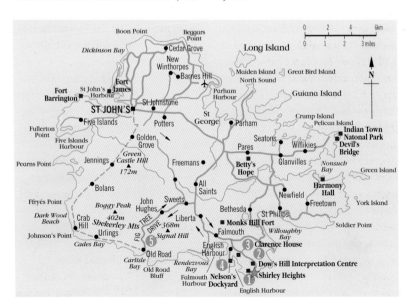

The Bahamas

On 12 October 1492, Christopher Columbus discovered the New World. He is said to have made landfall on the Bahamanian island of Guanahani, which he named San Salvador. North and east of the Caribbean proper, the 700 islands and 2,000 plus cays which comprise the Bahama Islands lie scattered across 260,000sq km (100,000sq miles) of Atlantic Ocean. Only around 30 of the islands are inhabited.

Originally, the archipelago was named the Lucayans, after the local Arawak people; the word Bahamas comes from the Spanish *baja-mar*, meaning 'shallow sea'. These flat, barren, coral rock islands were ignored by the Spanish and claimed by the British, who under the leadership of William Sayle founded a Puritan settlement on Eleuthera in 1648. This initial settlement was a failure, but Sayle discovered a fine natural harbour on the adjacent New Providence island where a fort and city (later called Nassau) sprang up. Within a few years, however, it had developed into a buccaneer base frequented by the likes of Blackbeard and Jack Rackham. Finally, pirate-turned-governor Woodes Rogers was enlisted by the British government to bring the colony under control in the 1720s, curtailing the privateers' raids. During the American War of Independence, the islands proved a useful source of arms for the rebels, and afterwards they welcomed fleeing loyalists who arrived with their slaves to set up plantations.

Further fortunes were made from gunrunning during the Civil War, and from bootleg booze during Prohibition. Since World War II, the Bahamas have experienced a tourist boom concentrated on the islands of Grand Bahama and New Providence. The billion-dollar industry employs around two-thirds of the workforce, who do not pay taxes, thanks to the revenue generated by offshore finance and ships' registry fees.

GRAND BAHAMA

From a handful of sleepy fishing villages to a major holiday destination within the space of 30 years, Grand Bahama, the fourth largest Bahamanian island, is one of the region's top tourist spots. More than a million visitors come every year, lured by its miles of white sand beaches and duty-free shopping.

Grand Bahama Tourist Office
PO Box F40251, International Bazaar, Freeport. Tel: (242) 302 2000.

Bahamas Ministry of Tourism *PO Box N3701, Nassau. Tel: (242) 322 7500.*
Rawson Square Tourist Information Booth *Nassau. Tel: (242) 326 9781.*
Also see: *www.bahamas.com*

Freeport/Lucaya

American entrepreneur Wallace Groves was the man behind Grand Bahama's transformation. The sprawling modern city of Freeport, together with its beach resort annexe, Lucaya, is very much based on the American model. Its broad boulevards, shopping malls and high-rise hotels are anything but Caribbean.

Garden of the Groves and Grand Bahama Museum

On the eastern outskirts of Freeport, this lush 5ha (12 acre) garden was laid out in honour of Mr and Mrs Wallace Groves. It is landscaped with over 5,000 varieties of flowers, shrubs and trees, pools fed by miniature waterfalls, meandering paths and plenty of quiet corners. Within the grounds, the Grand Bahama Museum highlights local history with displays of Stone Age Lucayan artefacts, pirate treasure, marine life exhibits and Junkanoo costumes used in the annual Christmas to New Year Festival.
Midshipman Rd. Tel: (242) 373 5668. Open: daily 9am–4pm. Admission charge to gardens; free admission to museum.

International Bazaar

A 4ha (10 acre) shoppers' paradise, the architecture here could best be described as 'international bizarre'. It was built in 1967 as the brainchild of a Hollywood special effects set designer, and houses an international cast of boutiques and stores which sell everything from French perfumes and Swiss watches to Japanese cameras and Irish linen. Local souvenirs are on sale in the Straw Market.
W Atlantic Drive, at W Sunrise Hwy. Open: Mon–Sat 9am–6pm.

Port Lucaya

This $10-million, 2.5ha (6 acre) site is Grand Bahama's latest shopping, dining and entertainment complex.
It overlooks a busy marina, and there are several good value cafés among the T-shirt stores and 'resort wear' boutiques.

If you fancy investigating marine life in the colourful coral reefs without getting your hair wet, get on to one of

Luxuriant vegetation and calm waters in Freeport's Garden of the Groves

the glass-bottomed boats that make regular departures from the port.
Royal Palm Way.
Open: Mon–Sat 9am–6pm.

NEW PROVIDENCE

Measuring just 11km by 34km (7 miles by 21 miles), New Providence became the chief Bahamanian island by virtue of its north coast harbour, site of present-day Nassau. This was the seat of the British administration until independence in 1973, and there is still a rather sleepy Anglo influence in historic Nassau, with its pith-helmeted policemen, horse-drawn carriages and shady squares. The development of flashy new resort areas in Cable Beach and Paradise Island (the latter linked to Nassau by a 457m/1,500ft toll bridge) places New Providence firmly in the frame as a major tourist stop.

Ardastra Gardens and Conservation Centre

Set in 2ha (5 acres) of tropical gardens, the Centre is home to around 300 birds and beasts from parrots, lemurs and jaguars to a troupe of marching flamingoes, the Bahamas' national bird.
2.5km (1½ miles) west of Nassau via Chippingham Rd. Tel: (242) 323 5806; www.ardastra.com. Open: daily 9am–5pm. Admission charge.

Cable Beach

The 'Bahamanian Riviera', this popular and busy sand beach fronts the island's biggest and best resort hotels, such as the 1,550-room Crystal Palace Resort and Casino. You'll find watersports galore, glass-bottomed boat trips and fine dining opportunities.
5km (3 miles) west of Nassau via West Bay St.

Fort Charlotte

Built to guard Nassau Harbour at the end of the 18th century, this sprawling, low-slung fortress affords grand views from its hilltop site. Above the moat, the white stone battlements are reinforced with cannons, while below ground you can visit the dungeons.
Off West Bay St, 1.6km (1 mile) west of Nassau. Tel: (242) 325 9186. Open: daily 8am–4.30pm. Admission charge.

Nassau

The busy cruise-ship dock is a couple of minutes' walk from the tourist office on Rawson Square and the town centre. On the west side of the square, there are

---

JUNKANOO

Cultural highlight of the Bahamanian year, the Junkanoo carnival kicks off on Boxing Day with a 'rush' (parade) through the streets of Nassau and Grand Bahama's West End. Costumed masquerades, decorated floats, dancers and bands are urged on by drums, whistles and home-made noisemakers in a national celebration with tangible African roots. The party atmosphere, beauty pageants and competitions climax in the New Year's Day Parade, but visitors can get a taste of Junkanoo year-round at the **Junkanoo Expo**, Prince George Dock, in Nassau, New Providence.

horse-drawn surreys for hire. The chatty drivers provide 45-minute tours for two. Across Bay Street, Nassau's main thoroughfare and shopping district, the pink-and-white House of Assembly faces Parliament Square (starting point for the Nassau Walk, *see pp54–5*). Several attractions lie a short distance from the town centre, easily reached by taxi or mopeds which can be rented near the dock. Cheap and frequent minibus services to Cable Beach leave from Bay Street and ferries make regular crossings to Paradise Island.

Pirates of Nassau

Interactive displays centred on Nassau's swashbuckling pirate era, including recreations of the 18th-century waterfront and a full-blown pirate ship. Sound effects and the smell of tar and rigging help to build the atmosphere.
Corner of George and King Sts.
Tel (242) 356 3759;
www.pirates-of-nassau.com.

Open: Mon–Sat 9am–6pm.
Admission charge.

Paradise Island

Known as Hog Island until 1962, the developer of this small island, linked to Nassau by a toll causeway (nominal charge for pedestrians), decided a name change was necessary in order to attract tourists. There are fine beaches to the west and to the north, exclusive hotels such as Disney's massive Atlantis resort, and the pretty Versailles Gardens and French Cloister on Paradise Island Drive, near the deluxe Ocean Club. The elegant 14th-century cloister, with its slim columns and carved capitals, was brought from the famous French pilgrimage town of Lourdes.
Paradise Island is just off the northeast coast of Nassau, reached by a toll bridge from Nassau. The bridge is walkable, and you can also get there by jitney bus from Bay Street, ferry from Prince George Wharf (daily 9am–6pm), or by water taxi.

The Yacht Harbour in Nassau

Walk: Nassau

Behind the busy port, which can handle up to ten cruise liners per day, Nassau's compact old town climbs uphill from the waterfront. It is easily explored on foot, and this relaxed walk combines a stroll down bustling Bay Street with visits to a small selection of historic sites.

Allow 2 hours.

Start at Parliament Square.

1 Parliament Square

The traditional hub of Bahamanian government, three sides of the square are bordered by the colonial-style, pink-painted buildings of the House of Assembly, the Ministry of Finance and the Supreme Court. In front sits an uncharacteristically young Queen Victoria flanked by cannons.
Head west (left) along Bay St.

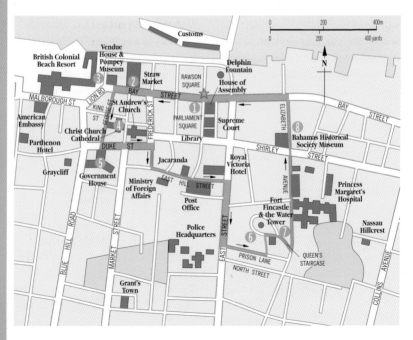

2 Straw Market

A visitor favourite for years, Straw Market houses almost 500 craft vendors under a 2,800sq m (30,000sq ft) canvas structure – light, airy and brimming with bargains, as always.
Continue west along Bay St.

3 Vendue House and Pompey Museum

Slave auctions were once held in this 18th-century building facing George Street. Today, the museum displays Bahamanian history exhibits and paintings by folk artist Amos Ferguson. These naïve renderings of colourful local scenes are now collectors' items.
Open: Mon–Fri 10am–4pm.
Admission charge.
Walk up George St to the corner of King St.

4 Christ Church Cathedral

Built on the site of the first church in the Bahamas, the graceful interior of the 18th- to 19th-century cathedral is lined with tall windows to catch the breeze. Wall plaques bear testament to a history of fevers and shipwrecks.
Continue up George St to Duke St.

5 Government House

The Governor-General's imposing residence sits at the top of shady George Street, clad in the official pink-and-white Bahamanian colour scheme. A statue of Christopher Columbus strikes a rakish pose on the steps.
Walk east (right) on Duke St. Just past St Andrew's Church take the steps up to East Hill, site of the blue-painted Friendship sculpture, given by the people of Mexico. Turn left along East Hill St, right on East St, then turn left up Prison Lane.

6 Fort Fincastle and the Water Tower

Dating from 1793, the fortress with its sharp-nosed prow never actually fired a shot in anger. It was, however, a useful lighthouse and signal station. Climb up on to the cannon-lined turret and sloping 'deck' for views of the harbour. For a real panorama, take a trip up the 38m (126ft) Water Tower.
Open: daily 9am–5pm.
Free admission.

7 Queen's Staircase

Take the famous 66-step staircase down to Princess Margaret's Hospital and Elizabeth Avenue. The staircase was carved out of the limestone hillside by slave labour in the 18th century.
Walk left down Elizabeth Ave towards Bay St.

8 Bahamas Historical Society Museum

This modest Bahamas Historical Society Museum charts local history with the aid of period maps, paintings and photographs.
Tel: (242) 322 4231. Open: Mon, Tue, Thur & Fri 10am–4pm, Sat 10am–noon. Free admission (donations accepted).

Cruising

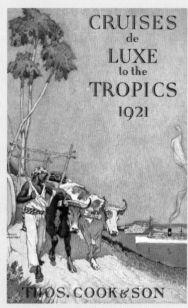

A vintage poster advertising cruises

Mankind braved the Seven Seas for thousands of years in the name of exploration, war and trade, but never as a leisure activity. Travellers generally had to work their passage, and the ocean-going part of any journey was extremely uncomfortable and frequently fraught with danger.

A list of draconian regulations posted on board in 1849 exhorted early fare-paying passengers to 'rise at 7am unless otherwise permitted by the Surgeon'. Before breakfast they had 'to roll up their beds, to Sweep the Decks … and to throw the Dirt overboard'.

All this was to change with the 20th century. Cruising arrived as a popular pastime for the rich, and shipping lines rose to the occasion by building opulent floating palaces. During the height of the transatlantic cruising era in the 1920s and 1930s, magnificent liners, such as the *Aquitania*, the *Normandie* and the *Queen Mary,* set sail with several thousand passengers ensconced in unbelievable luxury. Life on board was one hectic round of deck games and dancing. Guests' appetites were primed by a spot of tennis or deck quoits, before tucking into meals from menus the size of telephone directories.

Though the great liners and 'golden era' of cruising may have faded away due to the combined effects of the Depression, World War II and jet air travel, cruising is still a popular way to travel.

In the 1960s a small cruise line emerged offering 'Fun Ships' with cruises to nowhere, and a few that puddled around islands close to Miami. They offered a taste of cruising at affordable prices. That small cruise line is called Carnival, and

Cruises around the Caribbean have been a popular and luxurious way of touring the scenic islands for decades

today they own more than 50 per cent of all cruise ships, flying under various brand names and styles.

Today, you can cruise as elegantly or as casually as you like. Take your tuxedo to sea or leave it at home. Travel with masses on a mega ship complete with ice-skating rinks, cyber-cafés and rock-climbing walls; or choose a smaller ship, perhaps with computerised sails, and travel to out-of-the-way ports of call.

The Caribbean still remains the most popular cruising destination. Its year-round climate boasts almost continual warm (very warm in summer) weather and a wide variety of ports from which to choose. Cruising is here to stay. The romance of sailing the seas simply will not die.

Barbados

A pear-shaped island measuring 23km by 34km (15 miles by 22 miles), Barbados lies around 150km (100 miles) east of the Windward island chain. It was noticed, but not settled, by early Spanish and Portuguese adventurers who named the island Los Barbudos, or 'the bearded ones', after its native banyan (ficus) trees which drop a curtain of aerial roots towards the ground.

Barbados was uninhabited when the British claimed it in 1625, though its favourable climate and rich soil were to make it one of the most successful colonies in the West Indies. The British ruled Barbados for over 300 uninterrupted years until independence in 1966, and their influence still lingers. Familiar place names abound, from Bridgetown's Trafalgar Square to the hilly Scotland district in the northeast. The national sport (and abiding passion) is cricket, and there is even a touch of a West Country accent in the lilting Bajan speech.

There is plenty to see and do around the island; the sights are spread out around the various districts, typically named after saints. The sheltered west coast is famous for its smart hotels and seamless strip of white sand; the surf-lashed and rocky east coast is more picturesque, but swimming is dangerous.

Barbados Tourism Authority
PO Box 242, Harbour Rd, Bridgetown. Tel: (246) 427 2623; www.barbados.org.
There is also a pierside information kiosk.

Bridgetown and environs

Over a third of the island's total population of 254,000 live in the capital, Bridgetown. This bustling town pivots around central National Heroes (formerly Trafalgar) Square, overlooked by a statue of Lord Nelson erected in 1813 (more than two decades ahead of its counterpart in London). Off the square is Broad Street, the main commercial thoroughfare. To the north, part of the mellow stone Public Buildings complex is occupied by the House of Assembly. Though the site only dates from the 19th century, the Bajan parliament is the third oldest in the Commonwealth (after Britain and Bermuda), founded in 1639. A short walk east, 18th-century St Michael's Cathedral was rebuilt on the site of the original mid-17th century church. To the south of the square, the Chamberlain Bridge crosses the Careenage (a finger of sea) to a handful of pleasant cafés facing the waterfront.

Barbados Museum

Laid out in the old military prison, which formed part of the British garrison (*see Garrison Savannah, below*), this museum traces Bajan history through the ages. Collections of Amerindian artefacts, military memorabilia and exhibits relating to sugar production and slavery are displayed in a series of old cells. There are antique maps, portraits and photographs, a children's section and natural history displays.
St Anne's Garrison, 1.5km (1 mile) south of Bridgetown.
Tel: (246) 427 0201;
www.barbmuse.org.bb.

Open: Mon–Sat 9am–5pm, Sun 2–6pm. Admission charge.

Garrison Savannah

Once a British army parade ground, Garrison Savannah is now home to the Barbados Turf Club. Twenty race meetings a year take place on Saturdays on the grassy course, which is also popular with joggers. Around the Savannah there is an interesting collection of 19th-century buildings, old barracks, and rampart ruins belonging to Charles Fort (built in the 17th century) and St Anne's Fort, begun in 1704 but never completed.

The distinctive red-painted Main Guard (also known as the Savannah Club) is being restored to house a reception centre though there's not much to see inside.
Off Garrison Hill (2.5km/1½ miles south of Bridgetown).

The Promenade in Bridgetown

Barbados

Barbados

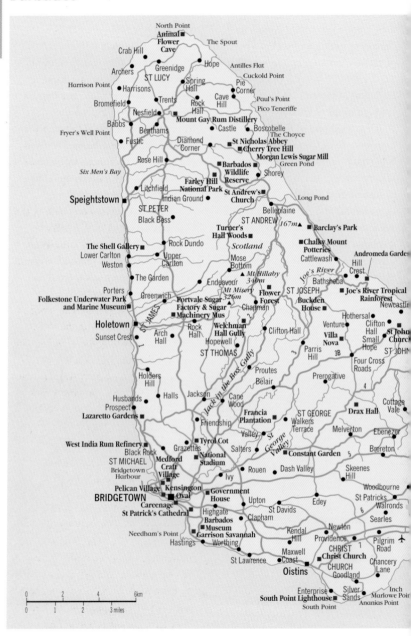

North Point
Animal
Flower
Cave
The Spout
Crab Hill
Archers
Greenidge
ST LUCY
Hope
Antilles Flat
Cuckold Point
Harrison Point
Harrisons
Spring
Hall
Pie
Corner
Bromefield
Trents
Rock
Hall
Cave
Hill
Paul's Point
Pico Teneriffe
Nesfield
Mount Gay Rum Distillery
Castle
Boscobelle
The Choyce
Babbs
Benthams
Fryer's Well Point
Fustic
Diamond
Corner
St Nicholas Abbey
Cherry Tree Hill
Morgan Lewis Sugar Mill
Rose Hill
Green Pond
Six Men's Bay
Barbados
Wildlife
Reserve
Shorey
Farley Hill
National Park
St Andrew's
Church
Speightstown
Litchfield
Indian Ground
Long Pond
ST PETER
Black Bess
Belleplaine
ST ANDREW 167m▲
Barclay's Park
The Shell Gallery
Rock Dundo
Turner's
Hall Woods
Scotland
Chalky Mount
Potteries
Andromeda Gardens
Lower Carlton
Weston
Upper
Carlton
Mose
Bottom
Cattlewash
Hill
Crest
The Garden
▲ Mt Hillaby
340m
Joe's River
Bathsheba
Porters
Folkestone Underwater Park
and Marine Museum
Greenwich
Endeavour
Mt Misery
326m
Flower
Forest
ST JOSEPH
Joe's River Tropical
Rainforest
Newcastle
Portvale Sugar
Factory & Sugar
Machinery Mus
Chapman
Buckden
House
Hothersal
Holetown
Sunset Crest
Rock
Hall
Welchman
Hall Gully
Clifton Hall
Clifton
Hall
St John
Church
Arch
Hall
Hopewell
ST THOMAS
Villa
Nova
Small
Hope
ST JOHN
Parris
Hill
3B
Four Cross
Roads
Proutes
Belair
Prerogative
Holders
Hill
Jackson
Cane
Wood
Husbands
Prospect
Halls
Francia
Plantation
ST GEORGE
Drax Hall
Cottage
Vale
Lazaretto Gardens
Friendship
Walkers
Terrace
Melverton
Ebenezer
West India Rum Refinery
Tyrol Cot
Grazettas
Valley
St
George
Valley
Brereton
Black Rock
National
Stadium
Salters
Constant Garden
Skeenes
Hill
ST MICHAEL
Medford
Craft
Village
Rouen
Dash Valley
Woodbourne
Bridgetown
Harbour
Ivy
Pelican Village
Kensington
Oval
Government
House
Upton
Edey
St Patricks
Walronds
BRIDGETOWN
Carenage
St Patrick's Cathedral
Highgate
Barbados
Museum
Clapham
St Davids
Searles
Needham's Point
Garrison Savannah
Kendal
Hill
Newton
Providence
Pilgrim
Road
Hastings
Worthing
Maxwell
Coast
CHRIST
CHURCH
Chancery
Lane
St Lawrence
Christ Church
CHURCH
Goodland
Oistins
Enterprise
Silver
Sands
Inch
Marlowe Poir
South Point Lighthouse
Ananias Point
South Point

0   2   4   6km
0   1   2   3 miles

Andromeda Gardens

This beautiful 2.5ha (6 acre) garden, perched on the east coast cliffs with glimpses of the bay below, was founded in 1954. Today, it is world-renowned for its variety of exotic species – orchids, heliconia, hibiscus, palms and cacti; and there are arches bound with fragrant stephanotis, frangipani trees and clouds of multicoloured bougainvillaea. Shaded corners reveal a mass of ferns and marvellous ornamental foliage.

Bathsheba, 16km (10 miles) northeast of Bridgetown. Tel: (246) 433 9384; www.andromeda.cavehill.uwi.edu. Open: daily 9am–5pm. Admission charge.

Animal Flower Cave

Twenty-seven deep steps lead down to this underground cave in the cliffs. Paddle about among the stalactites and stalagmites with a guide and watch yellow, orange and green sea anemones wave their tiny tentacles in the rock pools. There is also a swimming hole.

St Lucy District, 25km (17 miles) north of Bridgetown. Tel: (246) 439 8797. Open: daily 9am–5pm. Admission charge.

Barbados Wildlife Reserve

Set in 1.6ha (4 acres) of natural mahogany forest, this reserve provides a safe haven for green monkeys, or vervets, considered a pest by local farmers. Brick paths through the woods offer a chance to spot Brocket deer, lumbering tortoises, porcupines,

Conset Point · Coach Hill · Codrington College · Bell Point · Bayfield · Ragged Point · Thicket · Marley Vale · The Chair · Merricks · Kitridge Point · ST PHILIP · King George V Memorial Park · Sunbury Plantation House and Museum · Robinsons · Sam Lord's Castle · Shark's Hole · The Crane · Cobbler's Rock · St Martins · Salt Cave Point · Cobbler's Reef · ongor Rocks · assiah Street · Church Village · x Cross Roads · Blades · Mangrove

N

Three hundred years ago around 500 cane-crushing windmills existed in Barbados

agoutis and playful otters. There is also a walk-through aviary, reptile cages and a caiman pool, where these alligator-like creatures bask on the sunny banks. The Grenade Hall Signal Station by the car park was first used to keep an eye on the slaves in the cane fields, and then for spotting approaching ships.

Pleasantly shaded, well-signposted nature trails in the adjacent Grenade Hall Forest provide on introduction to the local flora.

St Peter District, 18km (12 miles) north of Bridgetown. Tel: (246) 422 8826. Open: daily 10am–5pm. Admission charge.

Codrington College

A magnificent driveway lined with lofty cabbage palms leads down to the elegant façade of this Anglican theological college. It was founded in 1745 and named after its benefactor, Christopher Codrington, a governor of the Leeward Islands, who was brought up in the original Codrington mansion, now the Principal's Lodge. The attractive grounds are open to view, with lily ponds and a woodland trail.
St John District, 17km (11 miles) northeast of Bridgetown. Tel: (246) 423 1140. Open: daily 10am–4pm. Admission charge.

Farley Hill National Park

A good spot to relax with a picnic, this national park is perched on a 274m (900ft) cliff with views over the rugged Scotland district. Laid out around the ruins of a 19th-century plantation house, the lovely landscaped grounds are planted with a wide variety of trees.
St Peter District, 17km (11 miles) north of Bridgetown. Tel: (246) 422 3555. Open: daily 8am–6pm. Admission charge for vehicles.

Morgan Lewis Sugar Mill

This 250-year-old sugar-grinding mill is the largest surviving windmill in the Caribbean region, complete with restored machinery and sails. It was in commercial use right up until 1944 (and is still in full working order), and affords panoramic views over the surrounding countryside.

A traditional-style wooden chattel house in Barbados

St Andrew District, 18km (12 miles) north of Bridgetown. Tel: (246) 422 7429. Open: Mon–Sat 9am–5pm. Admission charge.

St Nicholas Abbey

A gabled manor house built around 1650 to 1660, the 'abbey' is a rare example of Jacobean architecture in the Caribbean. The ground floor is lined with panelled walls (an old trick for concealing damp blisters in the tropics) and has been carefully restored. Furnishings include an ingenious multi-purpose 'gentleman's chair' which could cover all eventualities from toilet to reading stand. Walk around the gardens, and look in the bathhouse, equipped with a variety of hip baths.

St Peter District, 18km (12 miles) north of Bridgetown. Tel: (246) 422 8725. Open: Mon–Fri 10am–3.30pm. Admission charge.

Sunbury Plantation House

This comfortable 300-year-old plantation house first appears on a map dated 1681, and was a family home until 1985. It has survived several major hurricanes thanks to its sturdy 76cm (2½ft) thick walls. Fresh flowers and pot plants add a homely air to the reception rooms which contain mahogany furniture, antique silver and glassware, tall hurricane lamps and 19th-century engravings. Upstairs, there are displays of Victorian clothing laid out on four-poster beds. An old yam

HISTORIC HOMES

In addition to St Nicholas Abbey and the Sunbury Plantation House, Barbados has two other notable historic homes. **Tyrol Cot**, just north of Bridgetown, was home to former premier Sir Grantley Adams. Today it is the centrepiece of Barbados' first architectural heritage museum (Tel: (246) 424 2074. Open: Mon–Fri 9am–5pm. Admission charge). The elegant early 20th-century **Francia Plantation** is a working root vegetable plantation with terraced gardens overlooking the St George Valley (tel: (246) 429 0474. Open: Mon–Fri 10am–4pm. Admission charge).

cellar houses agricultural artefacts, domestic utensils and a cart and carriage museum; several historic conveyances are on show in the gardens. Refreshments are also available.

St Philip District, 15km (9¼ miles) east of Bridgetown. Tel: (246) 423 6270; www.barbadosgreathouse.com. Open: daily 9am–5pm. Admission charge.

Welchman Hall Gully

A favourite with plant lovers, this lush wooded gully was first laid out as a botanical walk in the 1860s. Abandoned for many years, it was rescued by the Barbados National Trust in 1962, and restored to a cool forest habitat with a 1.5km (1 mile) long path edged by towering bamboo, palms, nutmeg, clove and fig trees. Families of green monkeys crash about overhead in the late afternoon.

St Joseph District, 10km (7 miles) northeast of Bridgetown. Tel: (246) 438 6671. Open: daily 9am–5pm. Admission charge.

The unusual gabled façade of 17th-century St Nicholas Abbey

Bermuda

Britain's oldest colony and spiritual home of the ubiquitous knee-length shorts introduced by the British military around the beginning of the 20th century, the Bermuda Islands lie about 1,050km (650 miles) east of Cape Hatteras, North Carolina, in the Atlantic Ocean. Warmed by the Gulf Stream and protected by the world's most northerly coral reefs, seven of the 150 islands are connected by bridges and causeways to form Bermuda, which has three cruise-ship docks: Hamilton (the capital), St George and the Royal Naval Dockyard in the West End.

The islands were discovered by Spanish explorer Juan Bermudez in 1503, but settled only in the early 17th century by the British, after Sir George Somers was shipwrecked off St George's Island in 1609. Today, Bermuda is a popular summer season destination, delightfully British, with pubs and cricket pitches, luxuriant gardens and pretty pastel-painted cottages. It also tends to be the only port of call which allows passengers a full three or four days for exploring.

Bermuda Department of Tourism
*Global House, 43 Church St,
Hamilton HM12.*

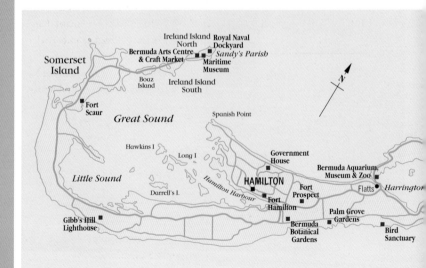

Visitors Service Bureau
Front St, Hamilton.
Tel: (441) 292 0023.
Also see: www.bermudatourism.com

Bermuda Aquarium, Museum, and Zoo

The Bermuda Aquarium offers a fascinating insight into the subtropical and tropical marine world. You'll find an amazing collection of brilliantly coloured sea creatures, from tiny fish and seahorses to penguins and Galapágos turtles, plus a natural history museum, and a Zoological Garden with a screeching, dazzling, entertaining collection of tropical birds and animals.
40 North Shore Rd, Harrington Sound. Tel: (441) 293 2727; www.bamz.org. Open: daily 9am–5pm. Admission charge.

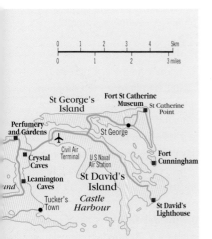

Bermuda Arts Centre and Craft Market

The Arts Centre occupies the former cooperage building, providing a display area for contemporary arts and crafts and travelling shows. You can watch local craftspeople and artists at work in the Bermuda Clayworks Pottery, and buy souvenirs such as handblown glass, quilts, wood carvings and traditional folkloric dolls.
Arts Centre. Tel: (441) 234 2809; www.artbermuda.bm. Open: daily 10am–5pm.
Craft Market. Tel: (441) 234 3208. Open: daily 9.30am–6pm.
Free admission.

Bermuda Botanical Gardens ('Camden')

Camden, the Bermuda premier's official residence, is set in these 14.5ha (36 acre) botanical gardens, founded in 1898. As well as formal gardens and an aromatic garden for visually impaired visitors, there are subtropical fruit groves, rare Bermuda cedars, banyan trees, a kitchen garden, an orchid house and an aviary.
169 South Rd, Paget (east of Hamilton). Tel: (441) 236 5921. Visitors Centre. Open: Mon–Fri 9.30am–3.30pm. Free admission.

Crystal Caves

Nature is at its most bizarre in these subterranean caves. Fantastic arrangements of stalactites and stalagmites create an eerie landscape

Bermuda

around underground saltwater lagoons. Pontoon bridges edge around the pools, which reach depths of 17m (55ft), though the water is so crystal-clear you'd think the bottom was just inches away.

Wilkinson Ave, off Harrington Sound Rd, Baileys Bay. Tel: (441) 293 0640.
Open: Apr–Oct daily 9.30am–4.30pm; check winter schedules. Admission charge.

Fort Hamilton

East of the city centre, Fort Hamilton, complete with moat, affords a panoramic view of the town and harbour. The Bermuda Island Pipe Band performs the Skirling Ceremony here, a distinctly Scottish affair complete with kilts, drums, dancers and bagpipes (check with the Visitors Service Bureau for details).

Off Happy Valley Rd. Tel: (441) 292 1234.
Open: daily 9.30am–5pm.
Free admission.

Fort St Catherine Museum

Fort St Catherine was founded in 1614 on the northeastern tip of the islands, where the survivors of Sir George Somers' shipwreck supposedly first set foot on Bermuda (*see p66*). It was constantly refortified against the threat of an invasion (which never came), and has battlements 8m (25ft) thick, plus powerful 18-ton muzzle-loading cannons. Inside there are excellent historical displays, an audio-visual tour of the islands' military outposts, a recreated cook

THE BERMUDA TRIANGLE

A triangular patch of the Atlantic Ocean bounded by Bermuda, Florida and Puerto Rico, this is the legendary graveyard for dozens of boats and planes, lost without trace. At least 100 ships and 1,000 sailors disappeared in the region during the latter part of the 20th century. One of the strangest incidents was the disappearance of five US torpedo bombers that took off on a routine two-hour patrol from Fort Lauderdale on 5 December 1944. Just before they were due to return, the patrol leader was asked to describe his position and replied, 'We don't know which way west is. Everything is wrong … even the ocean doesn't look as it should.' After radio contact was lost a search plane went out – it also disappeared. The US Navy commenced a five-year study, Project Magnet, to investigate the possibility of magnetic interference. Nothing was ever proved.

house and replicas of the British Crown Jewels.

15 Coots Pond Rd, St George.
Tel: (441) 297 1920. Open: daily 10am–4pm. Admission charge.

Hamilton

Bermuda's main cruise port and capital, Hamilton is a top shopping spot and an excellent base for trips around the island. The cruise-ship berths are a minute's walk from bustling Front Street. When you want to take a break from shopping there are several attractions to visit. On Church Street is the 19th-century **Bermuda Cathedral**. Close by, on the same street, **Bermuda National Gallery**'s collections of 15th- to 19th-century oil paintings and watercolours, alongside temporary exhibits, are housed in the modern **City Hall** (*Tel: (441) 295 9428; www.bermudanationalgallery.com. Open: Mon–Sat 10am–4pm. Admission charge*). On Parliament Street, off Front Street, on weekdays you can also visit the **Sessions House** (or Supreme Court), seat of the second oldest parliament in the world. A short walk west of Front Street brings you to Par-la-Ville Gardens and the Perot Post Office on Queen Street. Here you will find the **Historical Society Museum** with its eclectic collection of antiques and colonial memorabilia (*Tel: (441) 295 2487. Open: Mon–Sat 9.30am–3.30pm. Free admission*).

Maritime Museum

Housed in the old military buildings of the Keep Citadel, this interesting and informative museum illustrates Bermuda's long and colourful maritime history, from whaling and shipbuilding to piracy and rum-running. There are intricate model ships and nautical knick-knacks, gold and artefacts salvaged from wrecks displayed in the well-stocked Treasure House. You can also swim with dolphins at the **Dolphin Quest** attraction within the museum grounds.
Tel: (441) 234 1418; www.bmm.bm. Open: daily 9.30am–5pm. Admission charge. Dolphin Quest. Tel: (441) 234 4464; www.dolphinquest.org. Open: daily 9.30am–5pm.

Royal Naval Dockyard

The naval dockyard was developed in the 19th century, inspired by the Duke of Wellington's vision that Bermuda should become the 'Gibraltar of the West'. Heavily fortified and equipped with numerous ordnance buildings, barracks and a cooperage, the yard also boasts a splendid 30m (100ft) high clock tower, and the world's largest floating dry dock. The dockyard's new role is as a shopping, sightseeing, dining and nightlife complex.
Royal Naval Dockyard is 24km (15 miles) northwest of Hamilton. Ferries (30-minute journey time) depart from Hamilton, and there are efficient bus services.

Harbour scene at Sandy's Parish

Walk: St George

This picturesque port was the original capital of Bermuda (transferred to Hamilton in 1815), and has been immaculately preserved. It was designated a World Heritage Site by UNESCO in 2000.

Allow 2–3 hours.

Start at the replica of Deliverance.

1 Replica of *Deliverance*

This tub-like vessel is a faithful replica of the 17th-century ship, one of two sailing ships built by Sir George Somers' crew (*see p66*) in order to continue their journey to America.

Open: Apr–Nov daily 9am–5pm; reduced hours in winter. Admission charge.
Cross the bridge to King's Square.

2 Town Hall

To your right, a splendid colonial building dating from 1782, the Town Hall is home to the 'Bermuda

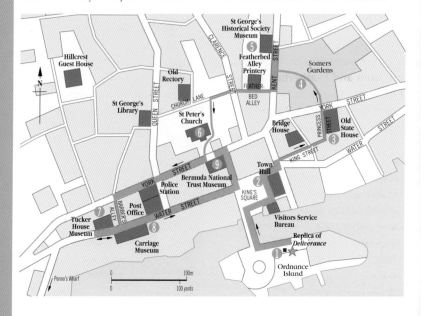

Journey' multimedia presentation.
Open: Mon–Sat 10am–4pm.
Free admission.
From the top right-hand corner of the square, head east (right) on King St.

3 Old State House
The Old State House was built in the Italian fashion by Governor Nathaniel Butler – who believed Bermuda was on the same latitude as Italy. It's now in use as a Masonic Lodge.
Open: most Weds 10am–3pm.
Free admission.
Walk north on Princess St.

4 Somers Gardens
Here lies buried the heart of Sir George Somers, who bravely sailed back to Bermuda from Jamestown, Virginia, to find supplies for the beleaguered colonists.
Cross Kent St to Featherbed Alley.

5 St George's Historical Society Museum and Featherbed Alley Printery
The Historical Museum, housed in a typical 18th-century Bermudan cottage, depicts bygone island life. Just around the corner, the Printery contains an antique press.
St George's Historical Society Museum.
Open: Mon–Fri 10am–4pm. Joint admission charge with Printery.
Featherbed Alley Printery.
Open: Mon–Fri 10am–4pm.
Head west across Clarence St on to Church Lane.

6 St Peter's Church
Take a good look around the gravestones (some are over 300 years old), before entering the church, built in 1713. The church treasure is displayed in the vestry.
Exit right on to York St, cross Queen St, turn left into Barber's Alley, and right on to Water St.

7 Tucker House Museum
Once home to one of Bermuda's most important families, this fine historic house is furnished with collections of cedar furniture, oil paintings, silver and antiques.
Open: Mon–Sat 10am–4pm.
Admission charge.
Cross Water St.

8 Carriage Museum
The first automobiles didn't arrive in Bermuda until 1946, so until then Bermudans got around in a variety of horse-drawn carriages.
Open: Mon–Fri 10am–4pm.
Admission by donation.
Head east on Water St towards King's Square and turn left to return to York St.

9 Bermuda National Trust Museum
Island history exhibits include an interesting section on Bermuda's role in the American Civil War. The island was a vital staging post for Confederate blockade runners involved in forwarding arms from Europe to the Confederacy.
Open: Mon–Sat 10am–4pm.
Admission charge.

Walk: St George

Cayman Islands

A group of three islands 240km (150 miles) south of Cuba, the Caymans are famous for banking, diving and tax-free shopping. These low coral islands are in fact the summits of underwater mountains and were spotted by Christopher Columbus on his fourth voyage in 1503. He named them Las Tortugas, 'the turtles', for their once abundant turtle population. The name did not stick, however, and the islands were rechristened Las Caymanas after the Carib Indian word for crocodiles.

The islands were ceded to Britain (together with Jamaica) in the Treaty of Madrid (1670) and were governed in tandem with the larger island. When Jamaica claimed independence in 1962, the Caymans chose to become a British Crown Colony. The largest and southernmost island of the group is Grand Cayman, home to around 26,000 of the 28,000 Caymanians. The rest live on the little sister islands of Cayman Brac and Little Cayman to the northeast.

Neatly laid-out George Town, where places are easy to find

Cayman Islands Department of Tourism
The Pavilion, Cricket Square, George Town, Grand Cayman. Tel: (345) 949 0623. Also see: www.caymanislands.ky

GRAND CAYMAN

An ever-popular stop with the cruising fraternity, Grand Cayman is relaxed, well-organised and virtually free of crime.

It is easy to get around, with local buses as well as taxis plying the northbound road from George Town, past the alluring white sand expanse of Seven Mile Beach to West Bay and covering the island's main attractions along the way.

George Town

As you step ashore at George Town, the tourist information booth offers helpful information and maps, including a *Historic Walking Tour* of the town. The main shopping areas

are around Fort Street and the Kirk
Freeport Plaza.

Atlantis Submarine

Non-divers should grab this
opportunity to experience the amazing
Cayman Wall from the comfort of their
own porthole. The colourful world of
corals and sponges is inhabited by a
breathtaking parade of weird and
wonderful marine life (*see pp74–5*).
George Town Harbour.
Tel: (345) 949 7700;
www.atlantisadventures.com.
Open: Mon–Sat 9am–3pm.
Admission charge.

Cayman Islands National Museum

Located in the Old Courthouse and
Jail, this museum houses a fine range of
exhibits charting the island's turbulent
history of pirates and wreckers, with
displays on shipbuilding, ropemaking
and turtle-hunting.
Harbour Drive, at Shedden Rd.
Tel: (345) 949 8368;
www.museum.ky.
*Open: Mon–Fri 9am–5pm, Sat
10am–2pm. Admission charge.*

Cayman Turtle Farm

This is the world's only commercial
green turtle farm. It plays a
conservation role by releasing a small
percentage of its captive-bred turtles
back into the wild. Here you'll find
thousands of turtles in varying stages of
development, from incubating eggs to
270kg (600lb) monsters. Hard-hearted

Grand Cayman

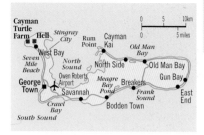

visitors can sample traditional Cayman
turtle dishes in the café. (NB: Turtle
products cannot be imported into the
USA or UK.)
West Bay Rd. Tel: (345) 949 3894;
www.turtle.ky.
Open: daily 9am–5pm.
Admission charge.

Hell

A well-trodden path, the road to Hell
ends up in a touristy spread of gift
shops and T-shirt sellers. The
weathered outcrop of ironstone here
is over 1½ million years old.
West Bay Rd, West Bay.

Stingray City

Touted as 'the best 12-foot dive in
the world', this extraordinary dive
and snorkel site brings its many
visitors within petting distance of
friendly stingrays, some of which
measure 1.8m (6ft) from wingtip to
wingtip. For those wary of entering
the water, boats allow passengers to
at least watch the graceful creatures
in the gin-clear sea.
North Sound.

Underwater world

'Ah, but you should be here at Carnival time,' they say. The brilliant colours, the swirling costumes, the pretty girls and vaguely sinister folkloric figures lend an exotic air to the Caribbean scene. Well, it is Carnival time every day of the year just below the surface of the glassy azure sea. The Caribbean region offers some of the most magnificent underwater scenery in the world, and it is yours for the price of a snorkel. In fact, you don't even have to get your feet wet, as flotillas of glass-bottomed boats and mini-submarines ferry visitors out over the reefs to view the colourful spectacle below.

Coral reefs are living entities built by limestone-secreting polyps. The forests of staghorn and elkhorn corals, delicate sea fans, feathers and whips of soft coral provide a fantastic backdrop for all manner of cute and bizarre sea creatures. Darting electric blue kissing fish (chromis), rock beauties, elegant grey angelfish and busy shoals of their black-and-yellow striped cousins, the sergeant majors, patrol beneath the waves. Sharp-beaked parrot fish crunch thoughtfully on chunks of hard coral, extracting the polyps and algae, while evil-looking eels lurk in crevices, their beady eyes also on the lookout for lunch. Decorator crabs – so-called for their habit of adorning their shells with an eclectic array of camouflage materials – scramble around the rocks surrounded by starfish, sea urchins and lobsters.

Top dive spots in the Caribbean include: Aruba, Bonaire and Curaçao

Inquisitive sharks and brilliant queen angelfish

Petrified forests of delicate coral are part of the scenery beneath the waves

(with a 5ha/12 acre underwater park), both in the Netherlands Antilles; reef and wreck sites in the Virgin Islands; the Bahamas; off Antigua; Barbados; and the French island of Martinique. Probably the most spectacular diving of all is in the Cayman Islands, where the famous Cayman Wall plummets 6,000m (20,000ft) straight down to the seabed. Grand Cayman's other claim to fame is 'Stingray City' in the sheltered waters of the North Sound, where divers and snorkellers can experience close encounters with huge semi-tame stingrays (*see p73*).

POPULAR DIVE SPOTS

ABC Islands – the Dutch Leeward Islands of Aruba, Bonaire and Curaçao (the latter features a 5ha (12 acre) underwater park) have many excellent sites.

Bahamas – the reef off Andros is spectacular.

British Virgin Islands – the wreck of the RMS *Rhone*, off Tortola, is arguably the best wreck dive in the Caribbean.

Cayman Islands – possibly the best scuba diving in the Caribbean. Swim with huge, semi-tame stingrays at Stingray City, or experience the 'north wall'.

Turks and Caicos – these islands are just opening up to scuba diving, with many new and colourful 'virgin' sites still being discovered.

Dominica

The 'Nature Island of the Caribbean', Dominica (pronounced Dom-in-ee-ker) is lush, green, mountainous and, almost invariably, wet. The Carib Indians called it Wai'tukubuli, meaning 'tall is her body', and Dominica's soaring interior scrambles up to a peak of 1,400m (4,500ft) from a base that measures just 47km by 26km (29 by 16 miles).

It is said that of all the Caribbean islands, Christopher Columbus would have least trouble recognising Dominica as it has changed so little. He landed here on 3 November 1493, a Sunday, hence its name. The warlike Carib inhabitants discouraged early European settlers and the wild jungle interior became a sanctuary for runaway slaves and for Caribs flushed from other islands by the colonists.

Despite a controlling British influence from 1763 until independence in 1978, Dominica retains few reminders of its former colonial masters. English may be the island's official language, but most of the locals speak French *patois*.

It has always been hard to make a living on Dominica, so the island has remained largely undeveloped. This has aided the survival of the Carib people, once widespread throughout the Caribbean, and is also a trump card in courting the ecotourism market.

Dominica Division of Tourism
Bay Front, Roseau. Tel: (767) 448 2401.
Information kiosks also at Dawbiney Place and Cabrits National Park.
Also see: *www.dominica.dm*

A saleswoman proudly displays her wares at Roseau market

Roseau

The island capital, Roseau reaches south of the Roseau River mouth in a grid of busy streets lined with weather-beaten wooden buildings. Sagging balconies, peeling gingerbread and rusty tin roofs give it a rather faded charm, but there is plenty of life in the open-air market by the river.

Set back from the waterfront, off King George V Street, the old cobbled market, **Dawbiney Place**, has been restored with a couple of tree-shaded benches and a tourist office kiosk beneath a cast-iron canopy.

The 19th-century stone **Cathedral of the Assumption**, reached via Church Street, sits on a small hill next to the manse. One of the island's best hotels occupies the remains of 18th-century Fort Young, once the town's main defence. Cruise passengers arriving at the Bayfront terminal in Roseau will find it a handy starting point for expeditions up into the Roseau Valley and to Morne Trois Pitons National Park in the central highlands.

Botanical Gardens

Within walking distance of the waterfront, this 16ha (40 acre) site nestles in the lee of Morne (Mount) Bruce on the edge of town. The gardens were established in 1890 on the site of a former sugar plantation. Today, the spreading lawns are a popular recreation area, with over 150 different plants and trees, including a giant baobab tree (Dominica's national tree) pinning a school bus to the ground exactly where it fell during Hurricane David in 1979. An aviary houses examples of both Dominica's indigenous and now endangered parrots: the purple-breasted Sisserou (or Imperial) and smaller red-necked Jaco parrot.

East of the town centre. Open: daily 6am–dusk. Free admission.

Trafalgar Falls

A popular side-trip from the capital, minibuses trundle to within a ten-minute walk of these beautiful 61m (200ft) falls. From the car park, there is a steep clamber up to the observation point, and sensible shoes are a must. The twin falls cascade down either side of a towering green-cloaked cliff face, bounce on the riverbed boulders and cool the air with their spray. Guides lead expeditions up to a second vantage point, or down to the river, which is strewn with black and orange rocks – dyed by traces of iron in the water.

Roseau Valley (east of town). Free admission; charge for guides.

Carib Territory

This 1,500ha (3,700 acre) territory on the Atlantic coast of the island was given to descendants of the Carib people in 1903. Around 3,000 Caribs live here, though most are mixed-race these days, and they have abandoned their simple thatched huts (*carbets*) in favour of wooden houses. Agriculture and fishing are the main occupations, and the Caribs still practise the traditional skills of canoe-making and basket-weaving. Mats, hats, baskets and bags are on sale throughout the island.

25km (16½ miles) northeast of Roseau.

Morne Trois Pitons National Park

Designated a UNESCO World Heritage Site, this 6,880ha (17,000 acre) national park encompasses a great tract of primordial rainforest, mountains, lakes and sulphur springs. To reach many of the sights, such as the seething, volcanic **Boiling Lake**, and sulphurous *fumaroles* (volcanic vents) of the **Valley of Desolation**, a serious full-day hike is required.

However, a new road into the park from Laudat gives access to the **Freshwater Lake** (at 762m/2,500ft above sea-level), and it is a pleasant two-hour return walk up to beautiful **Boeri Lake**. Alternatively, you could make tracks for the spectacular **Middleham Falls**. Island tours usually take in **Emerald Pool**, on the east side of the park. A ten-minute walk from the roadside through the forest ends up at a pretty water grotto which is topped up by a tiny waterfall. You can also see the park from a Rainforest Tram, which traverses the canopy from Laudat.

10km (6 miles) northeast of Roseau. National Park Information. Tel: (767) 448 2201. Rainforest Trams. Tel: (767) 440 3627; www.rfat.com. Admission charge.

PORTSMOUTH AND THE NORTHWEST

Although Portsmouth is Dominica's second largest town, it's dusty, sleepy and, with the exception of a couple of hopeful T-shirt sellers, apparently quite unaffected by the activity of the small modern Cabrits Cruise-Ship berth nearby. The town overlooks the thin black sand beaches and clear blue waters of wide, sheltered Prince Rupert Bay. Drake and Hawkins would stop off here to trade with the Caribs and resupply their ships, and the site was chosen for Dominica's first capital, later moved to Roseau.

Passengers disembarking here will find themselves immediately in the Cabrits National Park where tour buses and taxi drivers are available. The park is the only attraction in the immediate vicinity, though there is a picturesque cluster of brightly-painted wooden rowboats for hire at the mouth of Indian River to the south of town. Further afield, there are tour bus excursions to the **Northern Forest Reserve** on the slopes of Morne Diablotin, with an opportunity to

spot Dominica's rare Sisserou and Jaco parrots.

Cabrits National Park

On the north shore of Prince Rupert Bay, this national park incorporates the scattered remnants of Fort Shirley and assorted military outposts dating from 1765. The ruins of the 18th-century fort afford tremendous views across the bay, and there are various partially restored stone buildings dotted about the hillside lawns. Marked trails scramble up slippery, thickly wooded slopes to the crumbling Commandant's Quarters and other buildings swallowed up by the forest.
2km (1¼ miles) northwest of Portsmouth.
Open: daily 8am–5pm. Free admission.

Fisherman at Scotts Head village on Dominica's southwest coast

Grenada and Carriacou

Just 34km by 19km (21 by 12 miles), Grenada packs an astonishing variety of natural beauties into such a relatively small area. It is ringed by superb white sand beaches, while the mountainous interior climbs steeply past spice plantations, rainforests, gentle streams and cascading waterfalls to the island's highest point of Mt St Catherine (838m/2,757ft).

The 'Spice Isle of the Caribbean' lies at the southernmost tip of the Grenadines and is one of the world's chief producers of nutmeg, plus large quantities of mace (a byproduct of the nutmeg tree), cloves, cinnamon and ginger. Here you can literally smell spices on the breeze.

Columbus sighted the island on his third voyage in 1498. He named it Concepción, but future generations of Spanish sailors likened it to the hills of their native Granada, and the name stuck, albeit with a change of accent (it's pronounced Gra-nay-da) after a century of French occupation from 1650 onwards.

After years of fighting, the British finally gained control of Grenada in 1783, and kept it until independence in 1974. Grenada hit the world headlines in 1983, when a joint US-Eastern Caribbean rescue mission restored peace on the island after the leftist leader Maurice Bishop was deposed and subsequently executed in an uprising by members of his own party. Since then, things have returned to normal.

The island's tourist industry is one of the most carefully regulated in the region, with strict rules designed to preserve the environment; no building can stand taller than a palm tree, or be constructed less than 50m (165ft) back from the high-water mark. However, both the industry and the island suffered a devastating blow when Hurricane Ivan made a direct hit in September 1994. The 200kph (125mph) winds did terrible damage to both infrastructure and nature, but thankfully recovery has been swift. Almost all hotels are re-opened, and the only noticeable damage is the odd unreplaced roof or windblown tree.

Grenada Tourism Department
PO Box 293, The Carenage, St George's.
Tel: (473) 440 2279;
www.grenadagrenadines.com

St George's

Long-regarded as the prettiest harbour in the Caribbean, St George's is backed by a tight circle of hills formed by an extinct volcanic crater. The mouth of the harbour is guarded by the French-built **Fort George**. Behind the warehouses of the horseshoe-shaped Carenage (inner harbour), pastel-painted buildings cling to the hillside like limpets lining the precipitous streets.

The centre of St George's is located west of the harbour across the hill. You can reach it via the Sendall Tunnel which connects with the seafront Esplanade. If you visit on a Saturday, don't miss the brilliant spice and produce market on Market Square. It is one of the most colourful and photogenic in the whole Caribbean. There's a helpful tourist office right on the pier with a supply of free island maps and walking tour guides to the town (*see above*).

Grenada National Museum

This small museum is housed in the old French army barracks (built 1704), on the west side of the Carenage. It covers local history and culture from the earliest Caribs to the present day, including ancient artefacts, colonial knick-knacks and a look at events leading up to the 'friendly invasion' of 1983.

Monckton St off Young St. Tel: (473) 440 3725. Open: Mon–Fri 9am–4.30pm, Sat 10am–2pm. Admission charge.

Grenada and Carriacou

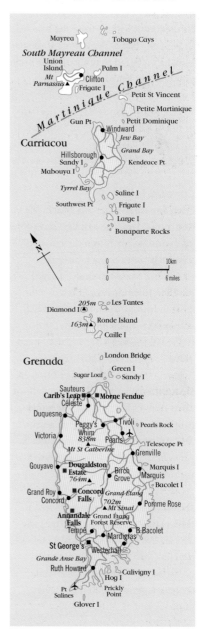

Carib's Leap

The 30.5m (100ft) high Carib's Leap cliff rears straight up from the sea. In 1651 the last of the island's Carib Indians preferred to jump off here and thus commit suicide rather than surrender to French colonists. This tragic event is also recalled in the name of the nearby settlement of Sauteurs (in French, 'the leapers').

32km (20 miles) northeast of St George's.

Concord Falls

There are three waterfalls here in the Concord Valley. The lowest is accessible by a winding road from the coast and is a popular spot on any tour of the island. You can swim in the natural pool for a nominal fee. It is a 25-minute hike up to the second fall, and another hour-plus to the 20m (65ft) tall top fall.

11km (7 miles) northeast of St George's.

Dougaldston Estate

Most of the island's spices are grown on this 324ha (800 acre) spice plantation, and although it has fallen on hard times, it still makes a fascinating visit. Inside the old wooden 'factory', you'll get an introduction to a wide variety of spices from cinnamon and cloves to tonka beans (a vanilla substitute) and allspice. All the while, a local guide explains the old-style processing methods. Mixed bags of spices only cost a couple of dollars, and make a great potpourri.

14km (8½ miles) north of St George's.

CARRIACOU

An occasional stop for smaller cruise ships, the diminutive island of Carriacou (13km by 8km/8 by 5 miles) is famed for its smuggling, its schooners, and the locals' tolerance for Jack Iron rum, a spirit so eye-swivellingly strong (160 per cent proof) that it causes ice to sink.

Hillsborough is the main settlement, with a bustling waterfront where you can see the graceful cedar schooners, locally built, and a Historical Museum in a restored cotton ginnery (mill) on Paterson Street. The beaches are gorgeous, but don't overdo the Jack Iron or you may miss your boat!

Open: Mon–Fri 9am–4pm, Sat 10am–1pm. Free admission.

Gouyave

Though *gouyave* comes from the French word for 'guava', this little clapboard town is the nutmeg capital of Grenada. Nutmeg was introduced to the island from the East Indies by British planters in the 1830s. As one of the world's top nutmeg producers, Grenada even features the nutmeg on its national flag. Take a tour around the **Grenada Nutmeg Cooperative** for the low-down on this spice and its waxy byproduct, mace. Afterwards, wander down to the beach for a view of the colourful fishing boats drawn up on the sand.

14.5km (9 miles) north of St George's. Grenada Nutmeg Cooperative. Open: Mon–Fri 8am–4pm. Admission charge.

Grande Anse Bay

This is the best beach on the island for day trippers. It comprises 3km

(2 miles) of gleaming white sands, with watersports, shopping and dining facilities.

5km (3 miles) south of St George's.

Grand Étang and Annandale Falls

High in the Central Mountain Range, the 12ha (30 acre) Grand Étang crater lake nestles in the forest, a cool 530m (1,740ft) above sea level. There are forest trails and walks around the lake – it takes about an hour to go all the way around. Keep an eye out for the mona monkeys introduced from West Africa over 350 years ago, and check out the exhibits in the roadside information centre.

Closer to St George's, the Annandale Falls and its visitor centre is another favourite stop along the road. The 9m (30ft) high waterfall splashes down into a bathing pool, bordered by a herb and spice garden. Park guides give narrated walks, and there are refreshments, crafts and spice stalls, and swimming as well.

11km (7 miles) north of St George's. Grand Étang Forest Reserve and Visitor Centre. Tel: (473) 440 2452.
Open: daily 8am–4pm & Sun when cruise ships are in. Admission charge. Annandale Falls Visitor Centre. Open: daily 8am–5pm.

Brightly painted boats drawn up on the sands of Grand Anse Bay

Grenada and Carriacou

Pirates of the Caribbean

The dastardly likes of Henry Morgan, Edward Teach (Blackbeard), 'Calico Jack' Rackham (so-called for his predilection for striped pants) and their cutthroat, rum-swigging, peg-legged cronies really did exist. And they caused havoc around the Caribbean region during the 16th and 17th centuries.

The region's early 'sailors of fortune' were known as *boucaniers* or buccaneers, a name derived from French hunter-adventurers who made a living from supplying passing ships with dried meat, cured in smokehouses called *boucanes*. Ambitious buccaneers soon abandoned the victualling trade to pursue richer pickings in the form of Spanish galleons. Laden with gold and precious gems from the New World, these floating treasure houses made tempting targets, and many buccaneers made the transition to a life of piracy via a spell as an officially sanctioned privateer. Armed with a government licence, or Letter of Marque, privateers were authorised to capture enemy ships in times of war. Once hostilities ceased, however, few felt inclined to resume a law-abiding lifestyle, and the buccaneer-privateers (also called freebooters or filibusters) soon turned buccaneer-pirates.

An exception was Henry Morgan, a notorious pirate-turned-privateer, who was appointed to rally the notorious Jamaican buccaneers during England's war with Spain in 1668. Morgan went on to capture and destroy the Spanish South American capital at Panama, then retired to his handsome estates

Though many have searched for buccaneer gold, little has been found

in Jamaica, where he was elected Deputy Governor, and became the scourge of his former comrades.

True pirates of the Caribbean owed allegiance to no one, however. They terrorised shipping from the Caribbean to North Carolina, occasional home of Edward Teach, better known as the notorious Blackbeard. Famed for roaring into battle with half a dozen pistols (three in each hand), and the pigtails of his beard spliced with lighted fuses, he was a frequent visitor to Port Royal, Jamaica, described in a London newspaper of the 1690s as the 'dunghill of the universe'. Other pirate hotspots included the Virgin Islands, and the tricky seas and secluded cays of the Bahama Islands.

But the golden age of Caribbean piracy was nearing its end. Governor Woodes Rogers arrived to clear up the Bahamas in 1718, the same year the Royal Navy caught up with Blackbeard. Defiant to the last, it is said Teach's decapitated body swam several laps around the ship before it sank. Calico Jack was surprised during a drunken revel in Jamaica, tried, hanged and left to rot on Rackham's Cay, off Kingston, in 1720. During the trial, two of his shipmates were discovered to be women, Anne Bonney and Mary Read, as ruthless a pair of bloodthirsty pirates as ever there was.

Tales of buried treasure and dastardly pirates abound in Caribbean folklore.

Although tales of hidden pirate treasure abound, little has ever been found. However, several sunken, treasure-laden Spanish galleons have been discovered, but most were victims of hurricanes and hidden reefs, not pirates. The most famous of the sunken galleons is the *Nuestra Señora de Atocha* found by Mel Fisher off the Florida Keys. Dive expeditions to the *Atocha* are available.

Guadeloupe and St Barthélemy (St Barts)

Shaped like a butterfly with two mismatched wings, the French-owned island of Guadeloupe is an unusual place. The western 'wing', Basse-Terre, is mountainous, rain-forested and dominated by the steaming Soufrière volcano. Grande-Terre, the northeastern 'wing', is flat and dry, its white-sand southern beaches proving a magnet for the trappings of the tourist industry.

GUADELOUPE

Sighted by Columbus in 1493, Guadeloupe was deemed one of the 'Cannibal Isles', and subsequently given a wide berth until 1635, when French settlers arrived to drive out the remaining Caribs. In terms of French priorities, the island played second fiddle to Martinique for years, though there was a brief moment of glory in 1794, when Guadeloupean *patriotes* overthrew the planters and installed a revolutionary government under Victor Hugues. (Martinique's planters and businessmen steadfastly maintained the pre-Revolutionary status quo.)

Guadeloupean slaves were freed, and Hugues erected the mandatory guillotine on the main square in Pointe-à-Pitre, where 300 enemies of the Revolution lost their heads. When Paris reintroduced slavery from 1802 until 1848, many freed Guadeloupean slaves preferred death to submission.

Guadeloupe has two cruise ports: the modest west coast capital of Basse-Terre; and the busier commercial centre of the island, Pointe-à-Pitre, located in the southwestern corner of Grande-Terre. From Basse-Terre, the Soufrière volcano is the most popular day trip. If you dock in Pointe-à-Pitre, you can opt for a day on the beach, or take a trip into Basse-Terre's Natural Park (*see p90*).

Guadeloupe Office Départemental du Tourisme

5 square de la Banque, 97163 Pointe-à-Pitre. Tel: (590) 82 09 30; www.francetourism.com

Grande-Terre

The main attractions on low-lying Grande-Terre are its beaches, and the best of these are found on the south coast between Gosier and St François. Gosier is the most touristy of the three seaside towns along this stretch. Both Ste Anne and St François are former fishing ports, though most of the fishing these days is done by

A rainforest path near the Maison de la Forêt in the Parc Naturel de Guadeloupe

tourists who enjoy the excellent sport fishing.

Fort Fleur d'Epée

Shaded by flaming Flamboyant (royal poinciana) trees, midway between Pointe-à-Pitre and Gosier, the ruins of these 18th-century coral rock fortifications afford fine views across the bay to Gosier, down the Basse-Terre coast to Pointe Capesterre, and across to the islands of Marie-Galante and La Désirade.
Open: daily 9am–5pm. Free admission.

Pointe-à-Pitre

Guadeloupe's main cruise-ship port and largest town, Pointe-à-Pitre is an unattractive port with congested streets and frenetic waterfront markets. However, you can relax in the cafés around place de la Victoire, the central gardens shaded by palm, mango and African tulip trees, cooled by fountains and edged by a clutch of venerable Colonial-style buildings.

Nearby, there is a small flower market outside the **Cathedral of**

Place St-François in the quiet Guadeloupe capital of Basse-Terre

St Peter and St Paul, with its iron frame bolted together like an elaborate Meccano set. Close to here, off rue Frébault, is the marvellous **Covered Market**, piled high with spices and sunhats, and staffed by garrulous stallholders.

A short walk away on rue Peynier, a pretty pink French townhouse with wrought-iron decorations and a double staircase houses the **Musée Schoelcher** (*Open: Mon–Fri 9am–5pm. Admission charge*). Here, you will find assorted mementoes of the famous French abolitionist who led the fight against slavery in the 19th century, together with collections of African ivories, model ships, ceramics and other curios.

Basse-Terre

The administrative capital of Guadeloupe is a small sleepy town tucked in the lee of the central highlands, about an hour's drive from Pointe-à-Pitre. Founded in 1643, Basse-Terre has several fine public buildings, a cathedral dating back to the 17th century, and the rambling ramparts of **Fort St Charles**, on the southern edge of town. Founded in 1650 and enlarged over the centuries, the fort now houses a small local history museum.
Museum. Open: daily 8am–4.30pm. Free admission.

Chûtes du Carbet

Fed by the Grand Carbet River, which originates in La Soufrière, these popular waterfalls come in three tiers. The 110m (360ft) high second spill is the most easily visited, just a 20-minute walk through the rainforest.
Northwest of St Sauveur.

Maison du Volcan

Perched on the forested slopes of La Soufrière above Basse-Terre, the Maison du Volcan acts as an unofficial visitor centre for the volcano, providing a potted introduction to vulcanism and the region's origins. The setting on the hill is lovely; there is an appreciable drop in temperature, and you can see a fair number of old Creole-style planters' houses nestled against the hillside.
St-Claude. Open: daily 10am–6pm. Free admission.

Parc Naturel de Guadeloupe
See pp90–91.

La Soufrière

The highest point in the Eastern Caribbean at 1,467m (4,318ft) above sea level, the sulphurous Soufrière crater is an eerie, nightmarish landscape of bubbling mud pools, bizarre lava formations and wisps of steam. Eruptions and major earth movements were noted in 1695, 1797, 1837, 1956 and 1976. Vehicles can venture as far as the Savane à Mulets, 305m (1,000ft) short of the crater. There are marked footpaths leading to the summit, and the uphill hike takes around two hours.

ST BARTHÉLEMY

More commonly known as St Barts, this pint-sized (23sq km/9sq mile) volcanic dot lies 200km (125 miles) northwest of Guadeloupe. It is the most chic spot in the Caribbean, with exquisite beaches, exclusive shopping and gourmet restaurants which will delight style-conscious Francophiles but not those on a budget.

First settled by French sailors from Brittany and Normandy, St Barts spent 100 years under Swedish rule during the 18th and 19th centuries, hence the name of the capital, **Gustavia**. Catch up on the island's history here at the **Musée de St Barthélemy** on the west side of the harbour (*Open: Mon 2.30–6pm, Tue–Fri 8.30am–12.30pm & 2–6pm, Sat 9am–noon. Admission charge*). And don't miss the delightful fishing village of **Corossol**, just north of Gustavia, a picture-book Breton community dropped into a tropical setting; some older ladies still wear traditional, frilly, starched Breton sun-bonnets. The best beaches are on the south coast at Anse du Gouverneur (no facilities) and Anse de Grande Saline; Anse des Flamands, in the north, has a couple of hotels.

St Barts Office Municipal du Tourisme
quai Général de Gaulle, 97133 Gustavia. Tel: (590) 27 87 27; www.st-barths.com

St Barthélemy

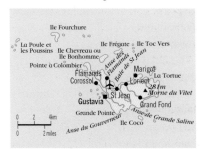

Tour: Guadeloupe

This 65km (40 mile) circuit out of Pointe-à-Pitre around the northern tip of Basse-Terre and Parc Naturel takes in spectacular rainforest scenery, a chance to visit one of Jacques Cousteau's top ten dive spots (by glass-bottomed boat) at Ilets Pigeon and a spot of rum tasting.

Allow a generous half-day (there is a suggested lunch stop at Deshaies if time permits).

Start in Pointe-à-Pitre.

1 Route de la Traversée

Once clear of Pointe-à-Pitre, this cross-island road skims westwards past sugar-cane fields lined with tulip trees (stunning in July), before climbing up into the 30,000ha (74,000 acre) **Parc Naturel** and crossing the Col des Mamelles. This pass affords stunning views of the aptly named twin volcanic peaks of Les Mamelles (The Breasts).

2 Cascade aux Écrevisses

Just inside the Parc Naturel, this waterfall gushes from the hillside near the road. A favourite picnic spot, sure-footed explorers can scramble around the boulders.
Continue along the D23.

3 Maison de la Forêt

Stop at the park information centre to pick up brochures on the local flora and fauna. There is a network of marked trails.

Open: Wed–Mon 9am–1.15pm & 2–4.30pm. Closed Tue. Free admission. At the end of the Route de la Traversée, turn south for Ilets Pigeon.

4 Ilets Pigeon

Frequent glass-bottomed boat tours depart for short trips out to this tiny island reserve just off the west coast. It is a bit of a detour, but the underwater panorama is spectacular, with visibility up to 24m (80ft), revealing superb corals and dazzling marine life.
Continue northwards along the coast.

5 Maison du Bois

Local woodcrafts are on show at this museum in the cabinet-making centre of Pointe Noire. Sections devoted to tools and domestic utensils from the pre-electric era include wicker lobster pots and hand whisks, plus machines for seeding cotton, grinding coffee and for building wheels and boats. There is a furniture showroom and a mini arboretum in the grounds.

Open: Tue–Sun 9.30am–5pm.
Admission charge.
Continue north to Deshaies, where there is a fine beach and a good Creole restaurant, Le Karacoli (see p173). The coast-hugging route then winds on past the popular surfing beach at Clugny to Ste Rose.

6 Musée du Rhum (Museum of Rum)

An exhaustive and detailed history of rum (with English translations) is enlivened by some evocative early 20th-century photographs of local merchants and craftspeople. These candid shots of the laundress and the sorbet maker, the milk ladies and the fish trap workers are reason enough to visit, but rum-lovers will also be offered an opportunity to sample the product after viewing a short film and taking a look at the various exhibits. A juice vat hewn out of a single tree trunk is particularly impressive.
Open: Mon–Sat 9am–5pm.
Admission charge.
The road runs inland from Ste Rose back to the Route de la Traversée. If you are short of time, return direct to Pointe-à-Pitre. Otherwise there is one last detour at Lamentin.

7 Ravine Chaude

The sulphurous natural hot springs at Lamentin are reputed to have healing and recuperative powers (especially after a long drive). But even if you do not fancy a dip, this is a good place to stretch your legs and enjoy a refreshing glass of punch before returning to the ship.
Take the N2 back to Pointe-à-Pitre.

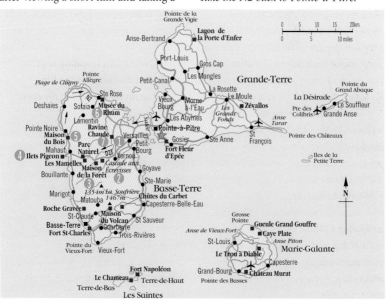

Jamaica

Over 1,100km (700 miles) south of Miami, Jamaica is the third largest of the Caribbean islands (11,424sq km/ 4,411sq miles), and a natural beauty with jungle-clad mountains, rushing rivers and superb beaches. Christopher Columbus reckoned it to be 'the fairest island that eyes have beheld'. Noël Coward, Errol Flynn, Ian Fleming (author of the James Bond novels) and a host of other famous devotees have lived here or found themselves returning time and time again, captivated by the island's physical beauty and the easy-going charm of its people.

When Columbus first landed here in 1494, the island was called Xaymaca ('Land of Wood and Water') by the peaceable Arawak Indians who inhabited it. The first permanent Spanish settlement was founded on the north coast in 1510, and the Arawaks were forced into slavery. Within a century, the estimated native population of around 100,000 had been wiped out. Many fell victim to European diseases; others were hunted for sport.

The English captured Jamaica from Spain in 1655, and set about turning the island into the world's largest sugar producer, using thousands of West African slaves who were bought and sold at slave markets in Kingston and along the north coast. From the latter part of the 17th century up until the abolition of slavery in 1834, the colonists flourished. And more than a few of them (such as Henry Morgan), made the switch to the 'respectable'

and luxurious planter's lifestyle after earning their fortunes on the high seas as buccaneers. Some slaves managed to escape and hide in the inaccessible mountain territory of Cockpit Country in the central west highlands. Known as Maroons, they waged a sporadic guerrilla war against the planters and

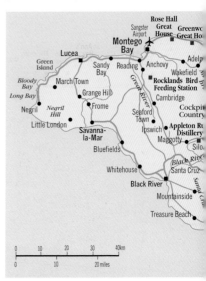

government. The most famous slave revolt was led by Sam Sharpe in 1831, today one of Jamaica's national heroes. Finally, in 1834, the Emancipation Act gave freedom to all slaves, though this only became reality after a subsequent four-year tied 'apprenticeship' period to the plantation. Former slaves claimed what land they could and turned to agriculture with the help of Christian missionaries. A century of political experimentation and the growing 1930s nationalist movement led to the creation of trade unions, political parties, and a new constitution in 1944. Jamaica was the first British colony in the Caribbean to achieve independence in 1962.

Jamaica's two main cruise ports are on the north coast, at Montego Bay and Ocho Rios, though some smaller cruise lines also use Port Antonio further east.

Jamaica Tourist Board

PO Box 67, Gloucester Ave, Cornwall Beach, Montego Bay. Tel: (876) 952 4425. PO Box 240, Ocean Village Shopping Centre, Ocho Rios. Tel: (809) 974 2582. (See also www.visitjamaica.com)

Kingston

The island's capital since 1872, Kingston sprang up after the old buccaneering base of Port Royal slid into the sea as a result of an earthquake in 1692. Today, this is the seat of government and business and boasts a population of over one million.

Kingston lacks charm but offers a handful of cultural attractions. A favourite escape from the downtown maelstrom is the short drive along the Palisadoes to the former site of Port Royal, where the ramparts of Fort

Jamaica

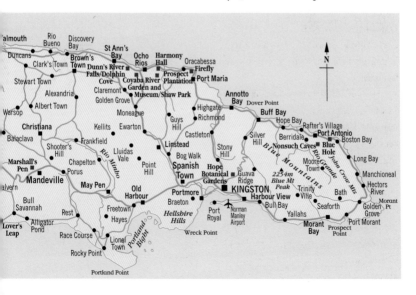

Charles afford views back to the Blue Mountains, and there is a small maritime and history museum.

Kingston Tourism Centre

PO Box 360, 2 St Lucia Ave, Kingston.
Tel: (876) 929 9200.
Also see: *www.jamaicatravel.com*

Bob Marley Museum

Reggae music fans should visit this memorial to Trench Town's most famous son, in the former Tuff Gong studio.
56 Hope Rd. Tel: (876) 927 9152.
Open: Mon–Fri 9.30am–5pm.
Admission charge.

Devon House

A restored 19th-century groat house with souvenir shops and restaurants in the stables. The interior boasts fine antique furnishings.

THE BLUE MOUNTAINS

Crowded into the eastern corner of the island, the spectacular Blue Mountains soar up to Blue Mountain Peak which tops 2,254m (7,402ft). The climb begins the minute you leave Kingston in a tortuous, winding squiggle all the way north along the Wag Water River to the Castleton Botanical Gardens, or northwest to the **Cinchona Gardens** at a breathtaking 1,676m (5,500ft). With a bird's-eye view of three deeply etched river valleys below, the Cinchona Gardens were originally laid out as a tea and cinchona plantation in 1868 (the bark of cinchona is used to make the anti-malaria drug quinine). The region is now noted for the Blue Mountain coffee, which experts rank among the best in the world. Make a visit to the coffee factory at Mavis Bank during the harvesting season (Sept–Feb), and purchase a hoard of the aromatic beans to take home.

26 Hope Rd. Tel: (876) 929 6602.
Open: Mon–Sat 9.30am–5pm.
Admission charge.

A mural representing Bob Marley, Kingston

Colonial-style Devon House, Kingston

Hope Botanical Gardens

Established in 1881, these 81ha (200 acre) botanical gardens provide an explosion of marvellous colour, shady paths, sweeping lawns, and elegant royal palms. There's also a restaurant and children's zoo to visit.
Old Hope Rd. Tel: (876) 927 1257.
Gardens. Open: 6am–6pm.
Zoo. Open: 10am–5pm. Admission charge to zoo; free admission to park.

National Gallery of Art

This is one of the best permanent displays of Caribbean art in the region, rich in oil paintings, drawings, sculpture and wood carvings. Notable names in the modern Jamaican art world include painters David Pottinger and Barrington Watson, and sculptors Christopher Gonzalez and Edna Manley.
Orange St (at Ocean Blvd). Tel: (876) 922 1561. Open: Tue–Thur 10am–4.30pm, Fri 10am–4pm, Sat 10am–3pm. Admission charge.

Spanish Town

The original capital of Jamaica for over 300 years, Spanish Town lies 22.5km (14 miles) west of Kingston. Though founded by the Spanish in 1523, the colonial-style Georgian stone buildings lend a distinctly British air to the town centre, where British naval hero, Admiral Rodney (inexplicably attired in Roman garb), strikes a commanding pose over the main square, known as The Park. On The Park a former governor's residence, the **King's House**, is home to a museum of folk crafts and colonial period furnishings, while 5km (3 miles) east on the road to Kingston, the **White Marl Arawak Museum** pays tribute to Jamaica's earliest inhabitants.
King's House. Open: Mon–Thur 9.30am–4.30pm, Fri 9.30am–3.30pm. Free admission.
White Marl Arawak Museum. Open: Mon–Fri 9am–4pm. Admission charge.

Jamaica

Doctor's Cave Beach was a fashionable health resort in the early 1900s

Montego Bay

'Mo' Bay' is Jamaica's second largest town, but number one in the island's tourism stakes. 'Montego' is derived from the Spanish *manteca,* meaning 'pig fat', from the days when sailors would come ashore here to hunt wild hogs. At the start of the 20th century it became fashionable to bathe at Doctor's Cave Beach, and the rest, as they say, is history.

Sam Sharpe Square, at the heart of town, is a short taxi ride from the cruise-ship dock. Adjacent to a statue of slave leader Sam Sharpe, The Cage is a former lock-up for slaves and drunks. The area around Montego Bay offers plenty of attractions, many of which can be covered by shore excursions.

Appleton Rum Distillery

Up in the hills of Cockpit Country, the Appleton Estate produces Jamaica's most famous rum. After a tour of the distillery, there are tastings and an opportunity to blend your own personal rum.

Siloah, 30km (20 miles) south of Montego Bay. Tel: (876) 963 9215. Open: Mon–Fri 9am–3.30pm. Admission charge.

Greenwood Great House

This was the Barrett family home, built by a relative of poet Elizabeth Barrett Browning in the early 19th century. Superb antique furnishings and musical instruments evoke the gracious plantation lifestyle.

26km (16 miles) east of Montego Bay. Tel: (876) 953 1077. Open: daily 9am–6pm. Admission charge.

RAFTING ON THE MARTHA BRAE

A river trip is just the ticket for a sweltering day, so take along your swimsuit for a 90-minute raft ride down the gentle Martha Brae River near Falmouth. Once clear of **Rafters' Village** (a distinctly tourist-orientated affair with shops, refreshments, and a swimming pool), the two-man, 30-foot bamboo rafts glide past tropical scenery with only the birds and butterflies for company.

Rafters' Village, 42km (26 miles) south of Montego Bay. Tel: (876) 952 0889. Raft hire daily 8.30am–4.30pm.

Rocklands Bird Feeding Station

Perched in the hills above the settlement of Anchovy, this is a great chance to get close to Jamaica's diverse and beautiful bird life. Hundreds of darting, chattering birds gather for the afternoon feeding sessions first initiated by 'bird lady' Lisa Salmon in 1958. Many of the diners are tame enough to feed from your hand.

14.5km (9 miles) south of Montego Bay. Tel: (876) 952 2009. Open: daily 2–5pm. Admission charge.

Rose Hall Great House

The most famous house in Jamaica – possibly the whole Caribbean – largely by virtue of its legendary mistress, Annie Palmer, who was also known as the 'White Witch of Rose Hall'. The 19th-century *femme fatale* is credited with bumping off three husbands and numerous slave lovers before being murdered in her bed. Guides in period dress lay it on thick as you tour the restored interior.

13km (8 miles) east of Montego Bay. Tel: (876) 953 2323. Open: daily 9am–6pm. Admission charge.

Port Antonio

Founded in 1723, this is the resort that time forgot – almost. Built on a point dividing two stunning bays, with the Blue Mountains in the background, Port Antonio's setting is truly fabulous. A booming banana boat port and resort at the beginning of the 20th century, the town's fortunes took a dive. Though the screen idol Errol Flynn bought Navy Island, near Port Antonio, and turned it into a Hollywood hideaway for his fellow stars in the 1940s and 1950s, Port Antonio has never fully recovered top resort status. Many of the buildings look very tired, but the waterfront has been spruced up by the construction of the **Errol Flynn Marina**, complete with oceanside promenades and a good restaurant.

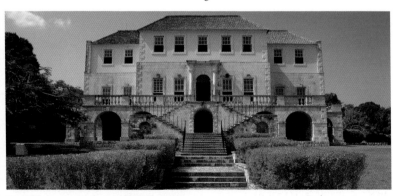

Rose Hall, home of *femme fatale* Annie Palmer

The local sights are pretty low-key, starting with the stunning **Blue Hole** (better known as Hollywood's Blue Lagoon). The **Nonsuch Caves** offer bizarre rock formations, and there are raft trips on the Rio Grande and trips to the pretty cascade of Reach Falls.

Ocho Rios and excursions

Midway along the north coast, 105km (65 miles) east of Montego Bay, the former fishing village of Ocho Rios has been given the full mass tourism development treatment and emerged as a seamless chain of hotels and burger franchises fringed by packed beaches. This is also Jamaica's busiest cruise ship destination. Duty-free shopping is within walking distance of the pier at the Island Village complex, but unless you want to spend the rest of the day on the beach, you will need transport to reach any of the local attractions.

Coyaba River Garden and Museum

The name comes from the Arawak word for 'paradise' and the museum occupies the grounds of the old Shaw Park Hotel, in turn built on the site of an ancient Amerindian settlement. It traces Jamaica's history and cross-cultural influences from the Arawaks and Spanish, through the colonial period, right up to the present day. Take time to admire the gardens, investigate the gallery and relax over a cup of home-grown Blue Mountain coffee or climb the picturesque Mahoe Falls, overlooked by a wooden walkway that

also affords a panoramic view over Ocho Rios.
Shaw Park Estate, 4km (2½ miles) west of Ocho Rios. www.coyabagardens.com. Open: daily 8am–5pm. Admission charge.

Dolphin Cove

Slick attraction where you can swim with and touch bottlenose dolphins in seawater pens fenced off from the ocean. Programmes range from a touch encounter to a swim with a dorsal pull; you can also swim with and pet nurse sharks and stingrays (the latter with barbs removed). Glass-bottom kayaking, boat rides, snorkel equipment and a shark show are included in the admission, and you can walk along the jungle trail to see parrots and iguanas, relax on the beach or have a meal or drink at one of the bars or restaurants.
Off the A1, 3km (2 miles) southwest of Ocho Rios. Tel: (876) 974 5335; www.dolphincovejamaica.com. Open: daily 8.30am–5.30pm. Admission charge.

Dunn's River Falls

Probably the single most popular outing for visitors to the island, these deliciously cool mountain falls tumble 183m (600ft) down to the sea over a series of easily climbable ledges. Check in your clothes and valuables at the ticket entrance lockers, and join the swimsuit-clad 'daisy chain' (a human conga line rallied by sure-footed guides) on the slippery route to the top. The ascent takes about 40 minutes.

Off the A1, 3km (2 miles) west of Ocho Rios. Tel: (876) 974 2857. Open: 8.30am–4pm, cruise ship days Wed–Fri 7am–4pm. Admission charge.

Firefly

Playwright and professional wit Noël Coward purchased this magnificent 305m (1,000ft) high crow's nest site in the 1940s, and must have spent much of his last 23 years admiring the incredible views. In fact, it is such a good lookout that buccaneer Henry Morgan is reputed to have used the tumbledown limestone building below the house as a shore retreat.

The interior of Firefly has been meticulously restored right down to Coward's silk pyjamas hanging in the wardrobe, and there are paintings, photographs and other memorabilia on display. Coward is buried in the garden beneath a plain marble tomb and a statue of him sits overlooking the coastline.

Off the A3, 34km (21 miles) east of Ocho Rios. Tel: (876) 997 7201. Open: daily 8.30am–5.30pm. Admission charge.

Ochos Rios

Harmony Hall

This attractively restored late-18th-century 'gingerbread' country house makes an inviting gallery for the works of contemporary Jamaican artists. Visiting exhibitions are a feature, and souvenir hunters will find a good range of top-quality craft items. There is also a bar, restaurant and garden terrace.

Off the A3, 6.5km (4 miles) east of Ocho Rios. Tel: (876) 974 2870; www.harmonyhall.com. Open: daily 10am–6pm. Free admission.

Prospect Plantation

The 405ha (1,000 acre) Prospect estate is one of Jamaica's finest working plantations, cultivating bananas, cassava, cocoa, pawpaws, pimentos and sugar cane among other crops. Entertaining narrated tours aboard an old-fashioned jitney (canopied open wagon) take around an hour, and include dramatic views of the White River Gorge, a stop at Sir Harold's Viewpoint for a panoramic vista of the coast, and an avenue of trees planted by such famous visitors as Charlie Chaplin and Sir Winston Churchill. If you fancy a spot of horse- or even camel-riding, call in advance and they will have a suitable steed awaiting you on your arrival.

Off the A3, 6.5km (4 miles) east of Ocho Rios. Tel: (876) 994 1373; www.prospect-villas.com. Open: daily for tours at 10.30am, 2pm & 3.30pm. Admission charge.

Jamaica

Martinique

Martinique is renowned for the beauty of its flora and its beaches. The island was spotted by Columbus on either his second or fourth trip, but not settled until 1635. Apart from a couple of brief foreign incursions during the 18th century, Martinique has remained indisputably French, and is a fully fledged region of France. French is the first (and often only) language, and the euro is the local currency.

Martinique is one of the larger islands in the Lesser Antilles (measuring 100km by 37km/62 miles by 23 miles), so plan your time ashore with care. A visit to the mountainous green heart of the island, dominated by the ominous volcanic bulk of Mont Pelée, is a 'must', while the capital, Fort-de-France, is a shopper's delight. To the south, rippling cane fields stretch off to the horizon behind some of those famous beaches.

Martinique Office du Tourisme
Immeuble Le Beaupré, Pointe de Jahem. Tel: (596) 61 61 77; www.martinique.org

Fort-de-France
Jardin Savane (Savane Gardens)
Clambering up the steep hillsides behind the Baie des Flamands, the capital's narrow streets pack closely around the attractive 5ha (12 acre) Jardin Savane on the harbour.

Nouvelle Bibliothèque Schoelcher (New Schoelcher Library)
Facing the top left-hand corner, the runaway Byzantine-Egyptian-Art Nouveau Bibliothèque Schoelcher was built for the 1889 Paris Exposition, and transported here piece by piece. It is named after Victor Schoelcher, a leading light in the 19th-century movement to abolish slavery.
Tel: (596) 702 667. Open: Mon 1–5.30pm, Tue–Thur 8.30am–5.30pm, Fri 8.30am–5pm, Sat 8.30am–noon. Free admission.

JOSÉPHINE
An 18th-century Martiniquan fortune-teller once read the palms of two cousins on the island and foretold that one would become an empress, the other 'more than an empress'. The former became Napoleon's Empress Joséphine. Her simple childhood home, **La Pagerie**, can be visited near Les Trois-Ilets (26km/16 miles south of Fort-de-France). The other was kidnapped by Barbary pirates and taken to Istanbul, where she became the Turkish sultan's favourite concubine, the Sultana Validé.

Musée Départemental d'Archéologie et de Préhistoire (Archeology and Prehistory Museum)
This museum houses exhibits on slavery, colonial life and some notable pre-Columbian artefacts. (*9 rue de la Liberté. Open: Mon 1–5pm, Tue–Fri 8am–5pm, Sat 9am–noon. Admission charge*).

Behind rue de la Liberté, the main shopping district is bordered by rue Victor-Hugo and rue Victor-Sévère. The Cathedral of St-Louis is here too, on rue Schoelcher.

If the beach is your prime objective, there is a convenient ferry service from the waterfront to four of the best beaches close to the capital. Plage Pointe du Bout offers a man-made strip of white sand lined with luxury hotels; Plage Anse-Mitan is also well-supplied with hotels and beach bars, and has good snorkelling; the narrow, sandy crescent of Plage Anse à l'Ane has plenty of shade and a couple of small hotel-restaurants; and Plage Grande-Anse is the most basic, with piles of fishermen's nets, laid-back beach bars and boats for hire.

Martinique

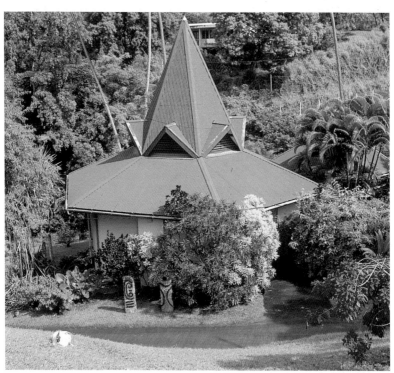

The Musée Gauguin at Anse Turin also displays work by local artists

Tour: Northern Martinique

An excursion into the spectacular Martinique rainforest should be one of the highlights of any Caribbean trip. The initial leg of this route from Fort-de-France follows La Trace, an inland forest road to St-Pierre, first carved through the undergrowth by Jesuits in the 17th century.

Allow 3 to 4 hours.

From Fort-de-France, head north towards Balata.

1 Sacré-Coeur de Balata

One glimpse at the *Montmartre martiniquais,* and you could be forgiven for thinking you are hallucinating. This mini replica of the famous Parisian basilica was erected in 1923 as a memorial to the dead of World War I.
Continue northwards.

2 Jardins de Balata

These glorious gardens are not to be missed. Massed hibiscus, poinsettias, bougainvillaea and plumes of red ginger glow in the sunlight, while glossy anthurium and pink torch ginger thrive in the shade. All around are ferns, fruit trees, spice bushes and variegated immortelles. Hummingbirds zip around the bushes.
Tel (596) 644 873; www.jardindebalata.com. Open: daily 9am–5pm. Admission charge.

3 The Rainforest

From Balata, the winding road continues up into the Pitons du Carbet, lined by a living curtain of ferns, bamboo and palms. Banana plantations cover the hillsides leading down to the coast.
Continue westward.

4 St-Pierre

Once the 'Paris of the Antilles', St-Pierre overlooks a splendid bay in the shadow of Mont Pelée. In the spring of 1902, after centuries of silence, Mont Pelée began to grumble. On 5 May, the volcano released a stream of mud and lava, but officials in the midst of an election campaign decided not to issue warnings. The governor arrived on 7 May, and urged people to leave, but only about 1,000 did.

Just before 8am on 8 May, the volcano erupted. A cloud of burning ash and poisonous gas at temperatures over 2,000°C (3,700°F) swept over the town and into the sea where it caused the water to boil. Around 30,000 Pierrotins were asphyxiated. Miraculously, Auguste

Cyparis, who was in the underground town lock-up, survived.

St-Pierre never recovered, and its present-day population of 6,000 live amongst the gaunt reminders of the cataclysmic eruption. You can explore freely around the ruins of the theatre, Cyparis' cell and the rebuilt cathedral (only the façade survived). The before-and-after photographs in the **Musée Vulcanologique** are well worth a look. *Rue Victor Hugo. Open: daily 9am–5pm. Admission charge. Follow the coast road south towards Fort-de-France.*

5 Musée Gauguin

The 19th-century French painter Paul Gauguin stayed on the beach here at Anse Turin for five months as he searched the Caribbean for a spot where he could live as a 'noble savage'.
Open: daily 9am–4.30pm.
Continue south to Le Carbet.

6 Le Carbet

This is said to be the spot where Columbus came ashore on his fourth voyage to the New World in 1502. French settler Pierre Belain d'Esnambuc definitely landed here, in 1635.
Continue south on this road to return to Fort-de-France.

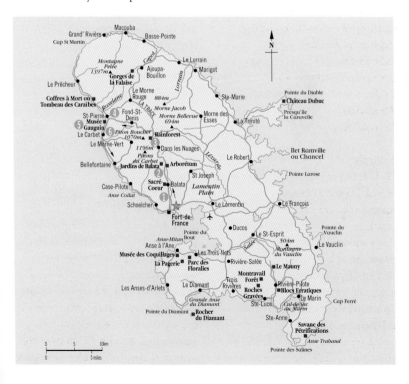

Slavery

The first Black African ever to set eyes on the Caribbean was Pedro Alonzo Niño. He was not a slave, but the navigator aboard the caravel *Niña*, one of three ships Columbus took on his first voyage to the New World.

The slave trade between West Africa and Europe was established by this time, and was in fact inspired by the Africans themselves. Domestic slavery of captured enemies was an accepted practice among African tribes, and they in turn sold their slaves to the Europeans in exchange

A notice of a slave sale

for manufactured goods such as textiles, glass and weapons.

As South America and the West Indies were colonised, and the native Amerindian population (the very first Caribbean slaves) were decimated by disease and ill-treatment, the search began for a replacement workforce to dig gold mines and tend the tobacco and sugar plantations.

The result was the infamous 'triangular trade'. Manufactured goods were shipped from Europe to be exchanged for West African slaves. The human cargo was then transported in appalling conditions on the notorious middle passage to the New World, where the ships were loaded with raw materials – sugar, spices, cotton, tobacco and rum – for Europe. It has been estimated that during the 250-year heyday of the Caribbean slave trade, as many as 40 million Africans were transported to the West Indies, the largest forced transportation of human beings in history. One in eight died on the middle passage.

Conditions were little better for the survivors on arrival. Sold at auctions like animals, slaves were then 'seasoned' with strict discipline. Beatings, brandings and the frequent use of neck chains, leg irons and other torturous devices were common. To further break their spirit and ties to African culture, families were split up and slaves were forbidden to speak in their native tongue. They worked 18-hour days, and children as young as five were put to work weeding and picking cane. Contemporary records show that up to 30 per cent of the slave population died every four years.

It was economics, not morals, that finally put paid to the slave trade. There were heroic abolitionists without doubt – Granville Sharp, Thomas Clarkson and William Wilberforce in Britain, and Victor Schoelcher in France, among them. But the introduction of sugar beet in Europe made the colonial trade less viable, and in 1838 (four years after the Emancipation Act) abolition finally became a reality in Britain. France followed suit in 1848.

Two excellent museums that explore the slave trade and the horrors of the middle passage are the Museum Kura Hulanda in Curaçao and the African Heritage Museum in San Juan, Puerto Rico. The first displays a life-size reconstruction of a slave ship that once sailed from the African coast. Other artefacts include musical instruments, sculptures and wooden masks.

Contemporary paintings present a stylised (and sanitised) view of slavery

Netherlands Antilles

The Dutch were important traders during the colonial era, and secured six possessions in the Caribbean: three in the Windward Islands and three in the Leewards. Sint Maarten in the Windwards is shared with France (see p124). The remaining Windward Islands, Saba and St Eustatius (known as 'Statia'), can only be visited by the very smallest cruise ships. Largely undeveloped, they remain rare oases of tranquillity. Over 800km (500 miles) due south, the Dutch Leeward Islands of Bonaire, Curaçao and self-governing Aruba (the ABC islands) lie off the coast of Venezuela.

ARUBA

This low-lying, scrubby island, some 32km by 10km (20 miles by 6 miles), had inauspicious beginnings. It was claimed by Spain in 1499, but subsequently rejected as an *isla inutila* (useless island), and it was ignored for over 100 years until the Dutch West Indies Company developed Curaçao. Aruba and neighbouring Bonaire proved useful for salt production and as ranches for cattle and horses. Few slaves were ever employed on the island, and it is therefore one of the rare places native Amerindians survived *in situ*, as can be witnessed in the faces of the local populace. The discovery of offshore oil in the 1920s led to an economic boom until declining prices turned the island towards tourism in the 1980s.

Though no longer technically a part of the Netherlands Antilles since gaining autonomy in 1986, Aruba

Netherlands Antilles

remains within the Kingdom of the Netherlands.

A taxi tour of the island takes just a couple of hours. Natural points of interest include the 165m (541ft) high **Hooiberg** (Haystack Hill) lookout point, and the Casibara and Ayo rock formations in the centre of the island.

On the north coast, the sea has carved the dramatic 30m (100ft) long, 8m (25ft) high coral rock **Natural Bridge** near Noordkaap, and there are huge dunes at **Boca Prins**. To the southeast, you can visit the ruins of the **Balashi Gold Mine** (some say the name 'Aruba' came from the Carib Indian words *ora uba* meaning 'gold was here'). You can also hike through the rugged surrounds of the **Arikok National Park** along well-marked trails. The most spectacular beaches, **Eagle** and **Palm**, edge the west coast north of Oranjestad.

Aruba Tourism Authority
PO Box 1019, 172 LG Smith Blvd, Oranjestad. Tel: (297) 582 3777; www.aruba.com

Oranjestad

Behind a cordon of duty-free shopping malls, old town Oranjestad (pronounced Oran-yeh-stat) is fun to explore. Some of the best examples of Dutch Colonial architecture are found along Wilhelminastraat.

Overlooking the bay, 18th-century Fort Zoutman houses local history exhibits in the **Museo Arubano** (*Oranjestraat. Open: Mon–Fri 8.30am–4.15pm. Admission charge*).

The **Archaeology Museum** displays Amerindian relics (*JE Irausquinplein 2A, near the post office. Open: Mon–Fri 8am–noon & 1–4pm. Free admission*).

Dazzling white sands at Rodgers Beach, Aruba

Netherlands Antilles

St Anna Bay in Willemstad

BONAIRE

Like Saba and Statia, only small cruise ships visit Bonaire. Most visitors come here for the diving, which is among the best in the world. Kralendijk is the island capital, with a population of 1,500. There's duty-free shopping on Breedestraat, a 19th-century fortress, Fort Oranje, and the small **Bonaire Museum** ten minutes' walk east of town (*Kaya J. van de Ree 7. Open: Mon–Fri 8am–noon & 1–5pm. Admission charge*). Around the island, there are salt pans in the south; and the 9ha (22 acre) **Washington Slagbaai National Park** in the north is notable for its bird life. Most of Bonaire's superb coral dive sites are off the protected leeward side of the island, easily accessible from Kralendijk.

CURAÇAO

This is the largest of the Netherlands Antilles (measuring 61km by 14km/ 38 miles by 9 miles) with a fine natural harbour. The Dutch landed on Curaçao in 1634, and swiftly transformed the strategically placed island into a major trading centre for European and South American merchants. Curaçao flourished, attracting a polyglot community who in turn developed the bizarre local dialect Papiamento, with strains of more than half a dozen European, South American and African tongues. To all appearances, Curaçao remains an exotic hybrid, a slice of picture-book Dutch in a spaghetti-Western setting, complete with cacti and tortured-looking *divi-divi* trees with branches forced back at 45 degrees due southwest by the cooling *Passatwinden* (tradewinds). Fans of the great outdoors should make for the arid but dramatic scenery of the Christoffel National Park (*see p147*).

Curaçao Tourism Development Bureau
PO Box 3266, Pietermaai 19, Willemstad. Tel: (5999) 434 8200; www.curacao-tourism.com

Willemstad

The cruise ship visitor's introduction to Curaçao's capital, and one of the

LANDHUISEN

It is reckoned that there were around 300 plantations on Curaçao by the 19th century, most of them with a fine country house in the grounds. Eighty of these houses remain, of which around one-third have been restored. A real highlight of any trip to Curaçao is a visit to the 18th-century **Landhuis Brievengat**, just north of Willemstad. *Open: Mon–Fri 9.15am–noon & 3–6pm. Admission charge.*

prettiest sights in the Caribbean, Willemstad's pastel-painted waterfront, the Handelskade, is a delight. It is said that a 19th-century governor first ordered the use of coloured paints on the red-roofed, gabled buildings as the dazzling whitewash was hurting his eyes. Today, it is a major tourist attraction.

Cruise ships dock in the Otrabanda quarter within walking distance of the town centre, the Punda, which is reached by the Queen Emma Bridge. (There is a free ferry when the 169m/555ft pontoon bridge is open.) On the waterfront, the late 17th-century Fort Amsterdam is now the governor's residence, and there's a floating market where Venezuelan schooners offload fruit and vegetables.

Curaçao Liqueur Distillery

The Curaçao Liqueur Distillery which occupies an old *landhuis* (country house) on the outskirts of town is a favourite stop for tour buses. A staple ingredient of any good cocktail bar, this famous sticky liqueur, which is produced from the peel of small, green oranges, comes in as many shades as the Willemstad waterfront, from the original orange to electric blue.
Tel: (5999) 461 3526. Open: Mon–Fri 8am–noon & 1–5pm. Free admission.

Curaçao Museum

For a spot of island history, return to the Otrabanda district and the Curaçao Museum, which displays Amerindian and colonial relics in a restored former seamen's hospital.

Van Leeuwênhoekstraat. Tel: (5999) 462 3873. Open: Mon–Fri 8.30am–4.30pm, Sun 10am–4pm. Admission charge.

Curaçao Seaquarium

The wonders of the deep (and not-so-deep) are superbly displayed in picture-window tanks. Included are more than 400 varieties of local marine life from fish to corals and sponges. Glass-bottomed boats sail out to the reef and there is a safe swimming beach here, too.
5.5km (3½ miles) east of Willemstad. Tel: (5999) 461 6666; www.curacao-sea-aquarium.com. Open: daily 8.30am–5.30pm. Admission charge.

Mikvé Israel-Emmanuel Synagogue

This is the oldest synagogue in the Americas. Founded in 1651, then rebuilt in the 18th century, it also has a small museum.
Columbusstraat. Tel: (5999) 461 1067; www.snoa.com. Open: Mon–Fri 9–11.45am & 2.30–4.45pm. Admission charge.

Bonaire slave huts, dismal and isolated

Puerto Rico

Over 1,600km (1,000 miles) southeast of Miami, Puerto Rico is the smallest of the four Greater Antilles islands, measuring around 177km by 56km (110 miles by 35 miles). Roughly rectangular in shape, it rises steeply from the developed coastal plains to a mountainous interior formed by the spine of the Cordillera Central, cloaked in lush tropical rainforest.

Arawak Indians called the island Borinquén, but Columbus rechristened it San Juan Bautista in 1493. Ponce de León, the discoverer of Florida, led the first group of Spanish settlers in 1508. He admired the *puerto rico* (rich port) of San Juan Bay and within a few years the island and the main settlement exchanged names. The Spanish held the island for 400 years, surviving hurricanes and frequent attacks by pirates and plunderers such as Sir Francis Drake, who sneaked past the town's defences to torch the Spanish fleet anchored in the harbour. Puerto Rican hopes for independence in the 19th century were dashed when Spain handed the island to the USA at the

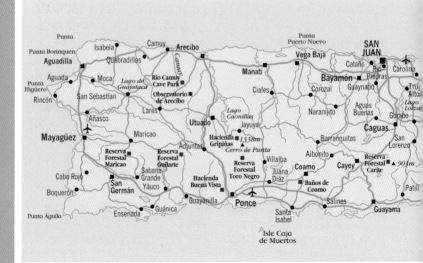

The massive fortifications of El Morro fortress in San Juan

end of the Spanish-American War in 1898. In 1917, USA citizenship was granted to Puerto Ricans, and the country is now a Commonwealth of the USA with an elected parliament run on the USA model.

The American influence is highly visible in the daily life of San Juan and in tourist areas, where English is widely spoken. Air-conditioned skyscrapers, chain hotels, gas-guzzling automobiles, American fashions, fast food and advertising are inescapable reminders of almost a century of US presence. However, the Puerto Ricans are proud and protective of their Latin origins. Catholicism, fiestas, the evening *paseo* (a pre-dinner stroll) and the clack of dominoes from *bodegas* and *tapas* bars lend Latin flavour to the streets of Old San Juan and quiet country villages.

Puerto Rico Tourism Company Information Center
La Casita, Calle Comercio, Old Town San Juan. Tel: (787) 722 1709; www.gotopuertorico.com

San Juan

The original Puerto Rico was well-named. It is now one of the world's top cruise destinations, home to more than 20 cruise ships, who disgorge over a million passengers every year. The pier is conveniently located a few minutes' walk from Old San Juan, a real slice of old colonial Spain with pretty balconied houses painted in yellow, white, fondant pink, powder blue and pistachio green. Some streets are paved with blue-grey bricks transported as ballast in ships bound from Spain. On the return voyage, these same ships would be loaded with treasures plundered from South America.

The settlement was actually founded in 1520, and construction of the great El Morro fortress on the western peninsula began 20 years later. The growing town was enclosed by 9m (30ft) thick fortified walls punctuated by round stone sentry posts called *garitas*. The modern city has expanded beyond the walls; east along the Atlantic coast to the modern hotel and beach resorts of Condado and Isla Verde; south to the university district of Rio Piedras; and west around the bay to Catano, where the **Bacardi Rum Plant** offers tours and tastings (*Open: Mon–Sat 8.30am–5.30pm, Sun 10am–5pm. Free admission*).

Within the compact Old Town area, the main shopping streets are Calle Fortaleza and Calle San Francisco, while a good place to find typical

LELOLAI

If you are staying over in San Juan at the beginning or end of your cruise, one way to experience Latin vitality and verve is a Puerto Rican country music and dance show. The LeLoLai folkloric performances celebrate centuries of European and Afro-Antillean rhythms and culture, and are staged in several San Juan hotels. For information and reservations, *tel: (787) 721 2400.*

Spanish-style bars and restaurants is the area around Plaza de San José. The main sights are covered in the walk around Old San Juan (*see pp114–15*).

Fort San Cristóbal

At the northeastern corner of the Old Town, this imposing 17th-century fort sprawls over an 11ha (27 acre) site, bordered by five bastions fitted with cannons trained over the Atlantic approaches. There is an interesting scale model in the museum, and the Devil's Sentry Box is home to a resident ghostly sentry.
Calle Norzagaray. Tel: (787) 729 6777. Open: daily 9am–5pm. Admission charge.

Luquillo Beach

This magnificent stretch of golden sand on the eastern Atlantic coast sweeps around a bay lapped by inviting turquoise waters. There is plenty of shade beneath tropical palms, while beach bars sell fresh coconut milk, piña coladas, soft taco rolls filled with crab or lobster, *alcapurrias*

(big banana fritters) and other delicious temptations. Quite simply – paradise!
Route 3, 48km (30 miles) east of San Juan.

Rio Camuy Cave Park
A popular day trip, the Cave Park offers tours into a 52m (170ft) high subterranean cavern adorned with monster stalagmites and stalactites.

A waterfall in the rainforest of El Yunque

Puerto Rico

It is part of one of the biggest cave networks in the Americas, and there are views of the River Camuy, one of the world's largest underground rivers.
Route 129 (KM18.9), 80km (50 miles) west of San Juan. Tel: (787) 898 3100. Open: Wed–Sun 8am–3.45pm. Admission charge.

El Yunque (Caribbean National Forest)
More than 450 billion litres (100 billion gallons) of rainwater fall on El Yunque (The Anvil) every year, so be prepared. However, all this precipitation has created a spectacular, rampant rainforest containing over 240 native species, including vines, epiphytes, giant ferns and all manner of brilliant flowers. The fauna is almost equally impressive, including the rare Puerto Rican parrot. Look for brilliant blue wings, a red forehead and green plumage.
Route 191, 64km (40 miles) east of San Juan. Tel: (788) 888 1800; www.fs.fed.us/r8/caribbean. Open: daily 7.30am–6pm. Free admission.

Walk: Old San Juan

The best way to appreciate Old San Juan is on foot. In addition to the major sights, there are numerous pretty streets, houses bedecked with window boxes and decorative iron grilles, small museums and several welcoming refreshment stops.

Allow a minimum of 3 hours, with stops.

Start at La Casita.

1 La Casita
This pink house, formerly the Customs House, is now the tourist office.
Proceed down the Paseo de la Princesa below the Old Town walls.

2 Raices Fountain
The Raices Fountain overlooking the harbour pays homage to the Taino Indian (Arawak), Spanish and African influences on Puerto Rican culture.
Continue along the walls.

3 Puerta de San Juan
Re-enter the Old Town by this massive city gate. Its studded wooden door dates from the 18th century.
Turn left uphill to Plazuela de la Rogativa. Take the ramp on the right into the gardens. Paths cut up to Casa Blanca on the right.

4 Casa Blanca
The daughter and son-in-law of island founder Ponce de León built the original fortified house here in 1521.

It contains a small museum of island history.
Tel: (787) 725 1454. Open: Tue–Sat 9am–noon & 1–4.20pm.
Admission charge.
Return through the gardens, and carry on up to the grassy headland and El Morro.

5 San Felipe del Morro
This stone fortress guards the entrance to San Juan Bay. It rises from the shore, with walls up to 6m (20ft) thick in places, and holds a maze of ramps and tunnels, lofty lookouts and dungeons. There are great views of the bay.
Tel: (787) 729 6754. Open: daily 9am–5pm. Admission charge.
Walk back across the headland and bear left on Calle Norzagaray, past the Cuartel de Ballaja, old Spanish barracks. Turn right up the steps of the Plaza del Quinto Centario.

6 Plaza de San José
A statue of Ponce de León stands on the square, but the real sight here is the

Iglesia de San José, a simple 16th-century church with a lavish altarpiece and monument to Ponce de León. Adjacent, the rickety **Pablo Casals Museum** displays cellos belonging to the famous musician.

Pablo Casals Museum. Tel: (787) 723 9185. Open: Tue–Sat 9.30am–5.30pm, Sun 1–5pm. Free admission.

Head a short distance west on Calle San Sebastián, and look for the entrance to the narrow street of steps on the left.

7 Escalinatas

These attractive old streets made up of flights of steps are lined with beautifully restored pastel-painted town houses.

Turn left at the bottom of the first stepped street, then right down the next step street and left again at the bottom. Rejoin Calle Cristo by the 19th-century cathedral and turn right. Continue along Calle Cristo.

8 Capilla del Cristo

At the bottom of Calle Cristo, this tiny 18th-century chapel with gilded carvings, ornate silver altar and oil paintings celebrates the miraculous escape of a horseman saved by divine intervention as he was set to plunge off the cliff.

Open: Mon, Wed & Fri 10.30am–3.30pm. Free admission.

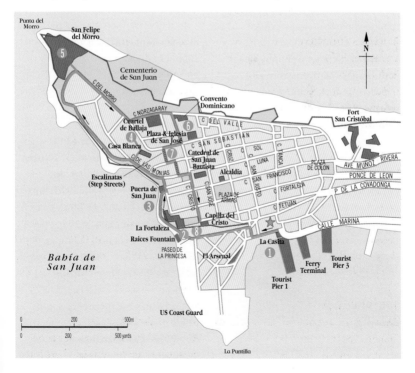

St Kitt's and Nevis

This brace of volcanic Leewards Islands is separated by a 3km (2 mile) wide channel known as the Narrows. St Kitt's is the larger of the two (at 176sq km/68sq miles), and is shaped like a tadpole, with the capital, Basseterre, on the southwest coast near the tail. A coast road circles the mountainous interior, dominated by Mount Liamuiga (1,156m/3,792ft), while another road runs down the tail, flanked on either side by white sand beaches.

The islands were sighted by Columbus in 1493, and he named the smaller one, Nevis, Nuestra Señora de las Nieves (Our Lady of the Snows) after its cloud-covered volcanic cone, which reminded him of a snow-capped peak. The larger island was christened St Christopher after Columbus' own patron saint and the patron saint of travellers. In time, both names were shortened to their present forms.

In 1623, St Kitt's was the first Caribbean island to be colonised by the English. And in 1626, in a rare (if brutish) display of common European purpose, English and French settlers massacred the Carib population at **Bloody Point**, a few miles west of Basseterre. Otherwise, the two colonialist powers fought intermittently for control of the islands' lucrative sugar industry until Britain gained the upper hand in 1783. St Kitt's and Nevis achieved independence in 1983.

St Kitt's Department of Tourism
Pelican Mall, Basseterre, St Kitt's.
Tel: (869) 465 4040;
www.stkittstourism.kn

Basseterre
The pint-size capital of St Kitt's stretches back from the wharf between the twin poles of The Circus and Independence Square. Plumb in the centre of The Circus, a Victorian clock tower serves as a public meeting place, surrounded by colonial buildings, with stone ground floors topped by wooden upper storeys and laced with gingerbread detail. Chickens strut around grassy Independence Square, which is overlooked by the Catholic church and Georgian houses. For a glimpse of old-time Basseterre, browse

Cannons point out to sea from the battlements of Brimstone Hill fortress

St Kitt's

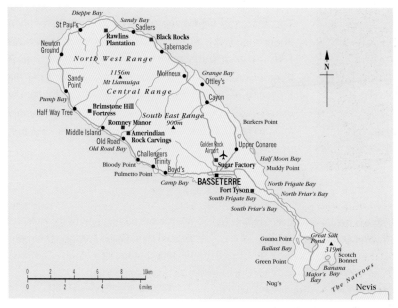

through the photographs at the
St Christopher Heritage Society, on
Bank Street (*Free admission*).

Brimstone Hill Fortress

Founded by the British in 1690, this
colossal 15ha (37 acre) fortress crowns a
244m (800ft) peak. Once known as the
'Gibraltar of the West Indies' and now a
UNESCO World Heritage Site, it was
considered impregnable until 8,000
French troops managed to breach the
2m (7ft) thick Magazine Bastion walls
after a month-long siege in 1782.
Main Rd, Brimstone Hill.
Tel: (869) 465 2609;
www.brimstonehillfortress.org.
Open: daily 9.30am–5.30pm.
Admission charge.

Rawlins Plantation

Set in quiet countryside in the
north of the island, this delectable
plantation house hotel is a fine,
quiet lunchstop.
15km (9¼ miles) northwest of Basseterre.
Tel: (869) 465 6221;
www.rawlinsplantation.com

Romney Manor

This modest 17th-century 'great house',
is now home to Caribelle Batik, one of
the island's most successful cottage
industries. On the drive up to the
house, a stone boulder features ancient
Carib petroglyphs.
Tel: (869) 465 6253;
www.caribellebatikstkitts.com. Open:
Mon–Fri 9am–4pm. Free admission.

Tour: Nevis

The 'Queen of the Caribbees', Nevis was one of the most prosperous islands in the Caribbean during the 17th and 18th centuries. Carpeted in cane fields and studded with elegant plantation houses (see box below), it grew rich from the profits of its slave market and developed into a regular social whirligig, welcoming the likes of Horatio Nelson, who married local girl Frances (Fanny) Nisbet in 1787.

Allow 2 hours.

This is a circular tour starting at Charlestown.

1 Charlestown

The engagingly low-key island capital (population 1,500) sports a riot of gingerbread decoration, a few craft shops and the interesting **Alexander Hamilton House** and **Museum of Nevis History**. This was the birthplace of 18th-century American statesman Alexander Hamilton, whose portrait graces US$10 bills.

Tel: (869) 469 5786. Open: Mon–Fri 8am–4pm, Sat 9am–noon. Admission charge.

2 St John's Fig Tree Church

Founded in 1680, and rebuilt in 1838, this pretty country church displays the wedding certificate of Horatio Nelson and Fanny Nisbet. (The couple were married on the Montpelier estate.) You can see the memorial plaque Fanny erected to

her parents on the right of the altar, and old tombstones concealed beneath the carpet in the aisle.

3 Horatio Nelson Museum

Near Charlestown's hot springs, and centred on Nelson himself, with everything from models of Nelson's Column in London, UK, to personal items owned by the great man.

PLANTERS' PARADISE

Many of the stately country houses built by rich Nevis sugar planters have been transformed into elegant hotels. If you feel like lunching in style, here are three suggestions:
Golden Rock Hotel: tropical forest setting with walking trails. *Tel: (869) 469 3346; www.golden-rock.com*
The Hermitage Inn: lovely antique-filled 18th-century house with terrace dining. *Tel: (869) 469 3477; www.hermitagenevis.com*
Montpelier Plantation Inn: beautifully restored stone house. *Tel: (869) 469 3462; www.montpeliernevis.com. Reservations advised.*

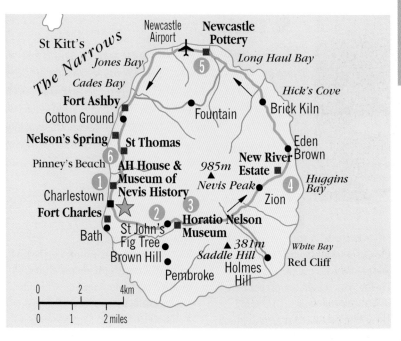

Open: Mon–Fri 8am–4pm, Sat 9am–noon. Admission charge.

4 New River Estate

Sugar production began at the 236ha (582 acre) New River plantation in the 17th century and continued right up until 1956. You can stroll around the mill ruins, slowly disappearing beneath the undergrowth.

5 Newcastle Pottery

Just past the Nisbet Plantation (now a very smart hotel), this roadside pottery workshop turns out simple handmade jugs, plant pots, candle shades and bowls decorated with bird and lizard figures made from local red clay. *Tel (869) 469 9746. Mon–Fri 10am–4pm.*

6 Pinney's Beach

The Fort Ashby ruins signal the northern extent of Pinney's Beach, which continues south in a sweep of golden sand all the way to Charlestown. You can stop at **St Thomas Anglican Church**, founded in 1643 and believed to be the oldest congregation on Nevis. Take a look around the memorials decorating the interior. One such glowing epitaph commemorates 14-year-old Elizabeth Lake, 'A Pious, Vertuous, Blamelesse, Spottlesse maid', who died in 1664.

Nevis Tourism Authority

Main St, Charlestown.
Tel: (869) 469 7550;
www.nevisisland.com

St Lucia

Arriving by ship is the best way to view St Lucia's famous Pitons, twin volcanic peaks which rise to a height of 732m (2,400ft) sheer out of the sea. The modern cruise-ship terminal, Pointe Seraphine, is a pleasant place to shop, but St Lucia's capital, Castries, is of little interest. The best day trip options are to head north for the beaches and Pigeon Island; or take a tour of the south like the one covered in the St Lucia Tour (see pp122–3).

St Lucia is one of the loveliest of all the Caribbean islands. This did not escape the notice of the British and French who fought almost continually over the island between 1674 and 1814. The decisive battle was a bloody affair at Morne Fortune in 1796, though it was another 18 years before the French finally ceded St Lucia to the British. In 1979 the island gained independence.

St Lucia Tourist Board
Suraline Bldg, PO Box 221, Pointe Seraphine, Castries. Tel: (758) 452 4094; www.stlucia.org

Castries
For a flourish of local colour, visit **Central Market** (*Mon–Sat 9am–5pm*) on Jeremie Street. Covered stalls sell straw hats, local crafts and food. Outside, fresh fruit and vegetables spill out on to the sidewalk. The other main sight is the **Cathedral of the Immaculate Conception**, on Derek Walcott Square.

Morne Fortune
The jungle-green hill climbs up behind Castries, dotted with houses. At the peak, in the grounds of Fort Charlotte, the **Inniskillen Memorial** (*Arthur Lewis Community College. Tel (758) 452 5507; www.salcc.edu.lc. Free admission*). commemorates the British fusiliers who captured the hill from the French in 1796. Further down, **Caribelle Batik** (*La Toc Rd. Tel (758) 452 3785. Mon–Fri 9am–5pm*) demonstrates the ancient art of batik.

Pigeon Island National Landmark
Pigeon Island was a former pirate lookout, 18th-century British naval headquarters and early 20th-century whaling station. For views south to the **Pitons** and north to Martinique, climb up to the ruins of **Fort Rodney**.
Gros Islet, northwest coast. Tel: (758) 450 0603; www.slunatrust.org.
Fort. Open: daily 9am–5pm; guided tours at 9.30am, 11.30am & 2.30pm. Admission charge.

St Lucia (*see pp122–3 for route*)

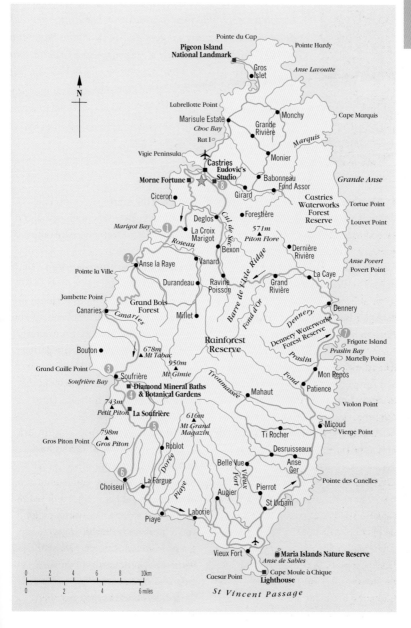

Pointe du Cap
Pointe Hardy
**Pigeon Island
National Landmark**
Gros
Islet
Anse Lavoutte
N
Labrellotte Point
Monchy
Cape Marquis
Marisule Estate
Grande
Rivière
Choc Bay
Marquis
Rat I
Monier
Grande Anse
Vigie Peninsula
Castries
Eudovic's
Studio
Babonneau
Fond Assor
Morne Fortune
Girard
Castries
Waterworks
Forest
Reserve
Ciceron
Tortue Point
Forestière
Louvet Point
Deglos
Marigot Bay
571m
Piton Flore
La Croix
Marigot
Dernière
Rivière
Roseau
Bexon
Anse Povert
Povert Point
Anse la Raye
Vanard
Pointe la Ville
La Caye
Durandeau
Ravine
Poisson
Grand
Rivière
Jambette Point
Canaries
Denbery
Dennery
Canaries
Grand Bois
Forest
Millet
Dennery Waterworks
Forest Reserve
Barre de l'Isle Ridge
Fond d'Or
Rainforest
Reserve
Frigate Island
Praslin Bay
678m
Mt Tabac
Praslin
Martelly Point
Bouton
950m
Mt Gimie
Fond
Mon Repos
Grand Caille Point
Diamond Mineral Baths
& Botanical Gardens
Soufrière
Patience
Violon Point
Soufrière Bay
Troumassee
Mahaut
743m
Petit Piton
La Soufrière
616m
Mt Grand
Magazin
Micoud
Vierge Point
798m
Ti Rocher
Gros Piton Point
Gros Piton
Roblot
Desruisseaux
Belle Vue
Anse
Ger
Dorée
Choiseul
La Fargue
Pierrot
Pointe des Canelles
Piaye
Augier
St Urbain
Vieux Fort
Piaye
Laborie
Vieux Fort
Maria Islands Nature Reserve
Anse de Sables
Caesar Point
Cape Moule à Chique
Lighthouse
St Vincent Passage

0   2   4   6   8   10km

0   2   4   6 miles

Tour: St Lucia

This drive down the west coast takes in beautiful bays and gardens, pretty fishing villages and what claims to be the 'world's only drive-in volcano' (see map on p121).

Allow around 5 hours.

Start at Castries.

1 Marigot Bay

Pretty as a picture, this bay has starred in several movies. Today, the idyllic sheltered harbour, encircled by steep forested slopes, plays host to a busy marina and resort.

2 Anse La Raye

Anse La Raye (it means 'Bay of the Rays' – stingrays in this case) is a typical fishing village of little wooden cottages and rusty tin roofs. The once plentiful rays have long since gone, but the fishermen are still here amid piles of nets and examples of local boat building on the beachfront. In the village itself

Drive to within a few hundred yards of La Soufrière's steaming, sulphurous pits

check out the murals decorating the church and playground walls; also the La Sikwe Sugar Mill on the edge of town.

3 La Soufrière town and the Pitons

Though the famous Pitons lie south of Soufrière, some of the best views can be enjoyed from the road as it runs down into town. A wander around Soufrière's main square will reveal the church and some gracious but rather tired old buildings laced with intricate, faded gingerbread decoration.

4 Diamond Mineral Baths and Botanical Gardens

Bring your swimsuit if you fancy a cure in these mineral baths, once enjoyed by Louis XVI's troops. The warm, milky-grey waters are fed by an underground spring from the Soufrière volcano. Rather more attractive are the luxuriant botanical gardens and waterfalls where the rockface and riverbed have been dyed orange by mineral deposits.

Marigot Bay's waters are almost too blue to be true

Tel: (758) 459 7565;
www.diamondstlucia.com.
Open: daily 9am–5pm. Admission charge.

5 La Soufrière

You can drive most of the way up to
La Soufrière's sinister and very smelly
sulphur springs, then walk the final few
yards to the bubbling pits. Guides point
out the various coloured mineral
deposits (green is copper oxide, purple
is magnesium and so on), and add
facts, figures and gruesome stories.
Tel: (758) 459 7686. Open: daily
9am–5pm. Admission charge.
Continue on around the southern coast.

6 Choiseul Arts and Crafts Centre

A marvellous place to buy unusual craft
souvenirs, this centre teaches young St
Lucians skills such as wood carving,
pottery and weaving, and many develop
into first-class artists.

Tel: (758) 459 3226. Open: Mon–Fri
9am–4.30pm.
Follow the coast road to Frigate Island.

7 Frigate Island

This observation point overlooks the
frigate bird-nesting grounds just off the
coast. From May to July, the great birds
(wingspan of over 2m/6ft) can be seen
coming and going.
Continue north to Dennery, then head
west on the cross-island road which runs
through the banana plantations back to
Castries.

8 Eudovic's Studio

Vincent Eudovic, a former teacher at the
Choiseul Arts and Crafts Centre, is one of
St Lucia's most important artists, and his
wood carvings are sold throughout the
island. This is both his home and studio.
Return to Castries following the main
road.

St Martin/Sint Maarten

This tiny island, with an area of just 96sq km (37sq miles), is one of the most developed in the Caribbean. The French/Dutch division dates from 1648. Local lore has it that a Frenchman and a Dutchman set off in different directions around the island, and the dividing line would be drawn between the point of their departure and where they met up.

The Frenchman fared rather better, gaining a 54sq km (21sq mile) portion of the island for 'La Belle France'. The Dutch muttered darkly about wily French tactics (the strategic deployment of a nubile French maiden to delay their man), but eventually accepted the lesser portion.

Despite this dual arrangement, the two halves of the island get along well.

There are no internal border controls, and English is widely spoken throughout the island, as are French and Dutch. Most cruise ships anchor off the Dutch capital of Philipsburg, an attractive shopper's paradise. If you plan on visiting both sides of the island, it is a good idea to head immediately for the French capital of Marigot, and enjoy coffee and croissants on the

St Martin/Sint Maarten

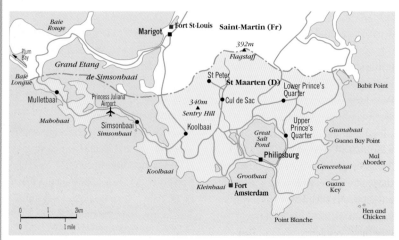

St Martin/Sint Maarten

A CHOICE OF BEACHES

Both sides of the island boast good beaches, but the beaches on the French (topless) side are generally quieter with few facilities.

The best is **Baie Longue**, on the west coast, with its neighbours, **Plum Bay** and **Baie Rouge**, close runners-up.

Busy beaches with good facilities on the Dutch side include **Mulletbaai** (Mullet Bay), **Simsonbaai** (Simpson Bay) and **Grootbaai** (Great Beach).

Great Beach's main advantage over the other two is that it is within walking distance of Philipsburg via Front Street.

harbour before returning to the bustle of Philipsburg.

Sint Maarten Tourist Office
Vineyard Office Park, 106 Buncamper Rd, St Maarten N.A. Tel: (599) 542 2337; www.st-maarten.com

Office Municipal du Tourisme de St Martin
Route de Sandy Ground, Marigot Waterfront. Tel: (590) 875 721; www.st-martin.org

Philipsburg
Philipsburg is the archetypal prettified West Indian town; its four main streets are intersected by *steegjes* (narrow alleys), painted in pastel colours and adorned with gingerbread woodwork. Front Street is a 16-block, open-air shopping centre, with a few fine old houses such as the lovely Pasangghran Royal Inn, a 19th-century former governor's residence, and the **Sint**

Maarten Museum. The museum's displays of buttons, bones, old musket balls and other relics salvaged from HMS *Proselyte*, which sank in Grootbaai (Great Bay) in 1796, are of passing interest, but the century-old house is an attraction in itself.
Sint Maarten Museum. Open: Mon–Fri 10am–4pm, Sat 10am–1pm. Admission charge.

Marigot
Marigot is much more laid-back than its Dutch counterpart, with sidewalk cafés, faded colonial buildings and a colourful morning market on the waterfront. This is a great place to relax over a late breakfast and admire the harbour view, look around the French speciality stores, and maybe take a hike up to the ruins of the 18th-century **Fort St-Louis**.

St Martin has many excellent beaches

St Vincent and the Grenadines

St Vincent and the 72km (45 mile) trail of tiny Grenadine islands stretching down towards Grenada is a top spot for Caribbean yachtsmen and other island hoppers. St Vincent is the largest of the islands at 344sq km (133sq miles), often referred to as 'the mainland' by the inhabitants of the 30 or so Grenadines, although many of these tiny cays are uninhabited.

St Vincent is explosively fertile – they say you could plant a pencil here and it would grow. The impenetrable green jungle barrier of the mountainous interior kept the Europeans at bay for years, and it provided excellent cover for warring bands of 'Yellow' (indigenous) and 'Black' (descended from runaway slaves) Carib Indians. After the Carib Wars ended in 1797, the British finally took control of the island where they grew sugar cane, arrowroot and cotton.

St Vincent and the Grenadines Tourist Office

Cruise-Ship Terminal, Bay St, Kingstown. Tel: (784) 457 1502; www.svgtourism.com

Kingstown

Behind the bustling waterfront, St Vincent's capital leads back into the steep hills that enclose the harbour.

THE GRENADINES

Of the eight inhabited Grenadine islands, only two receive much in the way of visits from cruise ships.

Just 14km (8½ miles) south of St Vincent, smart little **Bequia** (pronounced Beck-way) is fronted by Port Elizabeth on Admiralty Bay. Diversions include good craft and T-shirt shops, several pleasant waterfront eating places, and water taxis to the Princess Margaret and Lower Bay beaches.

The island of **Mayreau** (pronounced My-roo) makes Bequia look like a teeming metropolis. There are two wonderful beaches, or a steep hike up the hill to Dennis' Hideaway, where you can admire the view with one of Capt Dennis' lethal rum punches.

A walkway in St Vincent Botanic Gardens

On Tyrrell Street, the marzipan yellow and white **St George's Cathedral** contains a memorial to Major Alexander Leith, who put down the Carib Rebellion of 1795. Across the street, **St Mary's Catholic Cathedral** is a bizarre Neo-Gothic hotchpotch of black barley-sugar columns, pinnacles and turrets. Tyrrell Street runs out of town up to **Fort Charlotte**, with sweeping views to the Grenadines, and inland to the island's volcanic vertebrae.

Around St Vincent

Northeast of Kingstown, the fertile **Mesopotamia Valley** is a veritable market garden, growing bananas, breadfruit, coconuts, cocoa, nutmeg, arrowroot and more.

Day trips head along the west coast to the lovely **Dark View Falls**. On the way you'll glimpse the foothills of **La Soufrière**, the landmark 1,234m (4,049ft), still-active volcano which dominates the northern sector of the island.

St Vincent Botanic Gardens

Not to be missed, this is one of the oldest botanical gardens in the Western Hemisphere (founded 1765) and contains an amazing variety of weird and wonderful flora. Tip a guide to show you around oddities such as the sealing wax palm, the cannonball tree and the vast breadfruit tree, a descendant of the original plant brought to St Vincent by Captain Bligh in 1793.

Open: daily 6am–6pm. Free admission.

St Vincent and the Grenadines

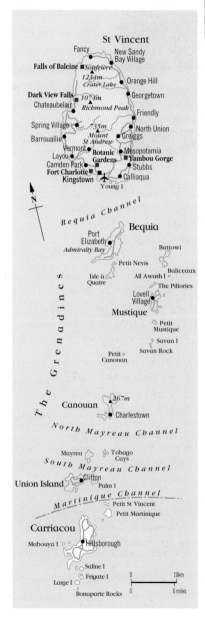

Tortola and the British Virgin Islands

The Virgin Islands archipelago lies scattered across 2,590sq km (1,000sq miles) to the east of Puerto Rico. Less than 1.5km (1 mile) separates the westernmost of the British Virgin Islands (BVI) from its nearest US cousin, St John, but the dotted line on the map does more than divide British and US territory; it denotes a complete change of style. Tourism is relatively new in the 60-plus islands, of which only 10 or so are populated. In fact, life is so laid-back you have to search pretty hard for a pulse.

Virgin Islands

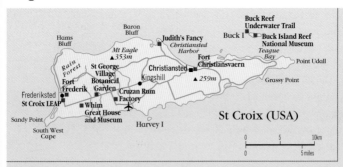

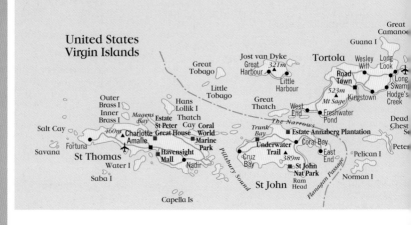

The first visitors were Arawak and Carib Indians, followed by Christopher Columbus in 1493, who was so taken by the islands' beauty he named them after the 1,000 virgins in the legend of St Ursula. After Sir Francis Drake sailed through the channel between the two in 1585, pirates and buccaneers found the islands an ideal hideaway. British planters introduced slave labour in the 18th century, but sailed away leaving the slaves behind. While other British islands sought independence in the 1960s, the BVI remained a Crown Colony. Economic ties with the US Virgin Islands (USVI) are strong (the US dollar is local currency), but for the time being, the inhabitants of the BVI are happy to remain separate and develop at their own pace.

Tortola/British Virgin Islands Tourist Board
2nd Floor, Akara Bldg, De Castro St, Road Town. Tel: (284) 494 3134; www.bvitourism.com

Tortola

The largest of the BVI (18km by 5km/11 miles by 3 miles), Tortola's capital, **Road Town**, is a small place with a folk museum and the pretty **JR O'Neal Botanic Gardens** (*Open: Mon–Sat 9.30am–5.30pm, Sun noon–5pm. Admission charge*).

Top of the island sights is **Sage Mountain National Park** at 523m (1,716ft), with fabulous views from the slopes of the high mountain, cloaked in primeval rainforest. Just north of here are lovely beaches at Cane Garden Bay and Apple Bay.

Virgin Gorda

Virgin Gorda was 're-discovered' by Laurence Rockefeller in the 1960s. He built a luxury resort here at Little Dix Bay, the first of several elegant developments. Virgin Gorda also offers a selection of stunning coral sand beaches. Here you'll find **The Baths**, a jumble of massive granite boulders forming grottoes and caves at the water's edge.

British Virgin Islands

Trinidad and Tobago

A twin-island state, Trinidad and Tobago are like chalk and cheese. Trinidad is the larger of the two, at around 80km by 61km (50 miles by 38 miles), and is the biggest of the Lesser Antilles islands. Literally a chip off the block of South America, which occurred as recently as 10,000 years ago, Trinidad breaks from the traditional Caribbean island mould with an industrialised oil-based economy and an unusually diverse multiracial population.

Located just 32km (20 miles) away, Tobago (*see pp136–7*) is much more like its Windward Island neighbours.

This tranquil, Caribbean idyll with its densely forested mountainous heart combines fishing and farming with a

Trinidad

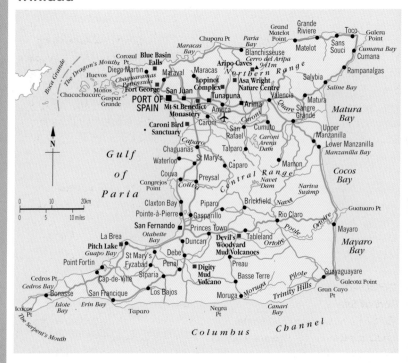

more developed, though strictly low-key, tourist industry concentrated on its beautiful beaches.

The Arawak Indians' Iere (Land of the Hummingbird) was christened Trinidad (Trinity) by Columbus in 1498, after the three peaks which dominate its southern bay. A Spanish colony founded on the island in 1592 was destroyed (but not supplanted) by Sir Walter Raleigh in 1595, and thereafter the Spanish paid scant attention to Trinidad. French settlers introduced sugar and cocoa plantations towards the end of the 18th century, but Britain seized the island in 1797 and it was officially ceded to the Crown in 1802.

With the abolition of slavery in 1834, African slaves deserted the plantations and East Indian indentured labourers were shipped in to take their place. Between 1845 and 1917, some 145,000 Indians arrived in Trinidad and many stayed on after their five-year term of labour, so that Indians and Africans now each account for approximately 40 per cent of the population. Chinese cane field workers added further to the racial melting pot, and together with migrants from South America, Europe and the Middle East, constitute the remaining 20 per cent.

TRINIDAD
Port of Spain
The hectic Trinidadian capital is the island in microcosm, a welter of modern skyscrapers and West Indian ginger-bread houses, pompous British colonial architecture, minarets and mosques.

On Frederick Street, markets and stalls sell everything from saris and bolts of Madras cotton to bootleg calypso tapes. Queen's Park Savannah is a huge, grassy breathing space with an eccentric collection of crumbling mansions nicknamed 'The Magnificent Seven'.

Botanical Gardens and Emperor Valley Zoo
These excellent gardens have spectacular flora and fauna.
200 Circular Rd. Tel: (868) 622 5343.
Open: daily 9am–6.30pm.
Admission charge.

National Museum and Art Gallery
An informative overview of Trinidadian history and culture, the museum tells the island's story through historical exhibits and artworks by local artists.
117 Frederick St. Tel: (868) 623 5941.
Open: Tue–Sat 10am–6pm, Sun 2–6pm.
Free admission.

Asa Wright Nature Centre
A 'must' on any island tour, this nature centre was established in 1967 at the Spring Hill Estate on the edge of the rainforest. The old plantation house has been turned into a hotel so nature lovers can actually stay up here and birdwatch from the balcony. Five trails lead off into the forest preserve which plays host to a stunning variety of native hummingbirds, butterflies,

Queen's Royal College – one of the 'Magnificent Seven', Port of Spain

CARNIVAL

Introduced by French settlers during the 18th century, the Trinidad Carnival (or 'Mas' – short for masquerade) is one of the biggest street parties in the world.

Hundreds of thousands of Trinidadians and visitors, many of whom have crossed the world just to be here for the carnival, pack the streets of Port of Spain for the main competitions and parades which start on the Friday before Ash Wednesday.

It is a veritable sea of glittering costumes, with the dancers and devils, bird-men and butterfly-women sashaying and strutting to the rhythms of steel bands and soca music pumped from speaker-laden trucks.
The Trinidad Carnival is an almighty but well-organised free-for-all with competitions galore, culminating in the Parade of Bands (Tuesday), which proceeds noisily along Aviapita Avenue and down Frederick Street to Queen's Park Savannah.

toucans and rare nocturnal oilbirds (or guacharos), once hunted by the Amerindians for their oil.
Near Arima, 20km (13 miles) east of Port of Spain. Tel: (868) 667 4655; www.asawright.org. Open: daily 9am–5pm. Admission charge.

Caroni Bird Sanctuary

This 182ha (450 acre) marsh, mangrove and lagoon sanctuary is home to the Trinidadian national bird, the scarlet ibis, as well as 157 other bird species, 80 types of fish, alligator-like caymans, sloths and great carpets of waterlilies. Tours are made by flat-bottomed boats, and the highlight (if time allows) is the spectacular dusk flight of ibises.
13km (8 miles) south of Port of Spain.

*Book via Nanan's Bird Sanctuary Tours.
Tel: (868) 645 1305;
www.nananecotours.com.
Admission charge.*

Chaguaramas Peninsula

Leased to the American military during
World War II, this peninsula is now
protected as part of the Chaguaramas
National Park. There is a clutch of
islands just off the western end of the
peninsula, one of which, **Gaspare
Grande**, boasts a cave complex adorned
with stalactites and stalagmites. Another
diversion is the **Military History
Museum**, a ramshackle but engaging
collection of artefacts that gives insight
into the American occupation (*Open:
daily 9am–5pm. Admission charge*).
*10km (7 miles) northwest of Port
of Spain.*

Fort George

This fortress-cum-signal station was
built in 1804. Fort George lies 20
minutes' drive from the centre of Port
of Spain, above the St James suburb.
At 335m (1,100ft) above sea level it
affords superb views over the island
capital, and across to the mountains
of northern Venezuela.
*St James, Port of Spain. Daily
10am–6pm. Free admission.*

Maracas Bay

The road north from Port of Spain,
known as Saddle Road, cuts a scenic
roller-coaster route through to the
coast. There are superb views along
the way, and the magnificent palm-
fringed sandy beach at Maracas Bay
is a popular spot at weekends, with
changing facilities and refreshments.
29km (18 miles) north of Port of Spain.

Pitch Lake

Worth a mention, though probably not
practical for day trippers (it is a good
six-hour round-trip from Port of
Spain), this 36ha (90 acre) asphalt 'lake'
is a truly bizarre natural phenomenon
and one of the largest deposits of its
kind in the world. It is said Sir Walter
Raleigh caulked his ships with the black
tar which seeps through the earth's crust
and forms a bouncy skin which you can
walk on. Around 91m (300ft) deep at its
centre, the level of the lake is slowly
dropping as the tar is mined for sale
around the world.
*60km (40 miles) southwest of
Port of Spain.*

Maracas Bay boasts one of Trinidad's best
beaches

Calypso

Music is the heartbeat of the Caribbean, and alongside Jamaican reggae, T&T's calypso and steel pan have become synonymous with region's musical output. Trinidad is the home of calypso, where it was first recorded in the 19th century, but its roots lie buried deep in the West African oral tradition of the griot, a travelling musician who brought news and gossip from village to village via song. During the slave era, Africans were forbidden to speak in their native tongues, but singing was permitted as a means of making work on the plantations more bearable. This chink in the planter's 'seasoning' process (see pp104–5) was swiftly turned into a means of keeping African story-telling traditions alive. Many of the songs had an allegorical slant, using animals or birds to hide real identities, and as such they were both protest songs and a way of passing on information. The very word 'calypso' may be derived from the West African *kai-so*, an expression of encouragement or approval.

Protest, information and gossip laced with humour are still the cornerstones of calypso today. The basic two-four or four-four rhythm does not permit an immense range of melodies, but calypso is strongly judged on its lyrical content, and its exponents are hailed as poet-performers in the West African troubadour tradition.

Calypsonians pull no punches. Their subject matter covers the spectrum from love, life and politics, to cricket or baldly stated warnings about AIDS. Styles vary from belligerent to raucous to downright raunchy. In competitions, other opponents are considered fair game and can be demolished with a few swipes of wickedly barbed humour.

The big names in calypso are partial to some pretty grandiose titles themselves: Lord Nelson and Lord Kitchener, Attila the Hun and the Black Stalin, among them. Perhaps the biggest of them all, the Mighty Sparrow's career has spanned over 30 years, and he has more Calypso Monarch (the top Trinidad Carnival calypso award) titles to his name than any other. Although calypso was largely a male preserve in its early days, the success of Calypso Rose (Rose Lewis), who in 1978 became the first woman to win the Monarch

Steel drums are the main instrument used in calypso

competition, paved the way for many more female performers, from Singing Sandra to Denise Plummer. These days, though, calypso takes something of a backseat to soca, its faster, more dance-oriented young cousin – and it's soca that you'll hear blasting through the streets at Carnival time.

But even more evocative of the Caribbean is the sound of the steel pan, which was invented in Trinidad in the 1930s when enterprising musicians stretched and tempered the lids of oil drums which had been discarded by the oil industry to create a brand new instrument. First played in the poorest sections of Port of Spain, the sound grew in popularity and soon replaced the tamboo-bamboo as the street music of Carnival, initially as a small 'pan around the neck' group of players, and now as 300-strong bands who tour the parade route with their instruments loaded on to converted flatbed trucks and makeshift trolleys.

TOBAGO

Trinidad's little sister makes a virtue of being different. Tobago is smaller, but prettier. The sedate lifestyle is so much more relaxing – perfect for holiday-makers who want to unwind – and there is little crime. Whereas Trinidadians tend to write off Tobagonians as being rather unsophisticated (though they still love to come here for weekend breaks), the people of Tobago pride themselves on being friendlier and more welcoming than the street-sharp 'Trickidadians'.

Trinidad and Tobago's political links originated fairly recently. A former pirate enclave turned prosperous sugar island, Tobago was grouped and governed with the Windward Islands until the late 19th century when the sugar industry collapsed. The island went bankrupt and was appended to up-and-coming Trinidad. Poor and underdeveloped, relying on subsistence agriculture for much of this century, Tobago has been rescued by the emergent tourism industry, which

Tobago

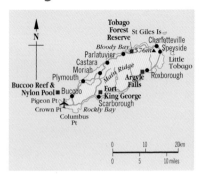

remains relatively low-key. The island's chief charms include unspoilt tropical forests and excellent snorkelling.

Scarborough

A sleepy little split-level town with a small cruise ship complex, Scarborough is the island capital. Down near the harbour, there is a colourful market, and the **Botanic Gardens** are a short walk away (*Open: daily 6am–6pm. Free admission*). Further uphill, remnants of the colonial era include the 1825 House of Assembly and Gun Bridge with railings made from recycled rifle barrels.

ROBINSON CRUSOE

Stop for a chat in Tobago and you might be regaled with tales of the island's favourite character, the shipwrecked mariner of Daniel Defoe's novel *Robinson Crusoe*.

Published in 1719, Defoe's novel was based on the real-life exploits of of a mariner, Alexander Selkirk, who was shipwrecked in the Pacific, off the coast of Chile. But Defoe moved his hero to Tobago. The Tobagans, in turn, have adopted Crusoe, and even named a cave on the northwest coast after him.

Fort King George

Perched on the hilltop 131m (430ft) above town, this 18th-century British fortress makes a terrific lookout point with views across to Trinidad. It now houses a small but informative **museum** of Amerindian and colonial artefacts in the Barrack Guard House.
Open site. Free admission.
Museum. Open: Mon–Fri 9am–4.30pm. Free admission.

Argyle Falls

Tobago's most visited waterfall, and the island's highest, at 54m (177ft) high, the Argyle is reached via a gentle 15-minute walk from the main road. There's a deep pool for swimming at the bottom, and you can climb the three tiers to the top.

Windward Rd. Tel: (868) 660 4154; www.argylewaterfall.com. Open: daily 9am–4pm. Admission charge.

Pigeon Point

This is the classic Caribbean beach, a strand of powder-soft white sand fringed with palms. There's a snack bar, changing facilities, watersports and glass-bottomed boat trips out to the superb **Buccoo Reef National Park**.

Open: daily 8am–5.30pm. Admission charge.

Tobago Forest Reserve

Another favourite spot for nature lovers, the Tobago Forest Reserve is the oldest of its kind in the Western Hemisphere, set aside by the British in 1764. Near Bloody Bay Lookout Site, the Main Ridge Forest Trail begins its winding descent through the rainforest to Bloody Bay, named after a gory ancient battle when the sand and sea turned red with spilled blood. Tropical birds and large, brilliant butterflies dazzle beneath the forest canopy and guides lead walks along the trails from Gilpin Trace.

Set above the northwest coast, near Parlatuvier.

Trindad and Tobago

Clear water, white sand and natural shade, if desired, on Pigeon Point Beach

US Virgin Islands

The 'American Paradise', the US Virgin Islands are a collection of some 50 islands and cays east of Puerto Rico. The three main islands are St Thomas and St John in the north, and St Croix (pronounced 'Croy'), out on a limb, some 64km (40 miles) due south. The American influence is all pervasive in St Croix and St Thomas, two of the most developed islands in the Caribbean. St John is an exception since two-thirds of its 41sq km (16sq miles) is a protected national park. (See map on pp128–9.)

Christopher Columbus anchored off St Croix on 13 November 1493 on his second voyage to the New World. The following day he set sail for the islands on the northern horizon and spent four days charting the jumble of islands he named Las Once Mil Virgenes (the 11,000 Virgins). The Spanish tried to settle St Croix shortly afterwards, but it was abandoned for over a century. Dutch, English and French colonists arrived next in 1625, but were ousted by the Spanish in 1650, who in turn were almost immediately evicted by the French.

Meanwhile, the Danish West Indies Company set up a permanent base on St Thomas in 1671, claimed St John in 1684, and set to work planting sugar cane, cotton and indigo estates. St Croix was bought from the French in 1733. St Thomas was declared a free port in 1724, and profited handsomely from the European conflicts being fought in the Caribbean. During the American War of Independence, Danish neutrality and St Thomas' free port

status initiated strong ties with the USA. An early attempt by the USA to buy the islands from the Danes in 1867 was vetoed by the islanders but in 1917, the collapse of the sugar trade finally persuaded the islands' inhabitants to opt for the USA bid.

ST CROIX

The largest of the Virgin Islands (212sq km/82sq miles), St Croix has two cruise-ship piers: **Christiansted**, the capital, accommodates smaller vessels, while big ships put in at **Frederiksted**, 27km (17 miles) west. Though 'Croy' is far behind St Thomas in the tourist development stakes, this is part of its charm. There are fewer crowds and the locals have more time to chat.

USVI/St Croix Tourist Office
PO Box 4538, 41A Queens Cross St, Christiansted, 00822–4538 USVI. Tel: (340) 773 0495.

Christiansted

A delightful small port settlement set back from the harbour and toy-town Fort Christiansvaern, Christiansted offers good shopping and some great little restaurants and bars. The settlement was originally founded in 1735, and there are still several 18th- and 19th-century buildings dotted about. The most notable of these is the **Steeple Building**, a former Lutheran church which now houses a modest museum of local history (*Open: daily 8am–4.45pm. Free admission*).

Offshore to the east of Christiansted, the 344ha (850 acre) **Buck Island Reef National Monument** offers the best beach on (or rather off) the island, with two underwater trails and excellent snorkelling and diving. Frequent boat services for the island leave from the docks in Christiansted.

Fort Christiansvaern

Bearing more than a passing resemblance to a rather large toy castle, this yellow and white fortress was largely completed between 1738 and 1749. It has been restored to its appearance circa 1830–40, with neat, green painted shutters and pyramids of cannon balls. On the upper storey, a small historical exhibition traces the origins of the fort.

Tel: (340) 773 1460; www.nps.gov/chri. Open: Mon–Fri 8am–4.45pm, Sat & Sun 9am–4.45pm. Admission charge (includes entrance to Steeple Building museum).

Cruzan Rum Factory

This is a favourite stop on the tourist trail in the western corner of the island. The modern factory was built in the grounds of the former Diamond Sugar Mill, although today molasses, the raw ingredient for rum, has to be imported. Half-hour tours trace the distilling process, followed by tastings.

Off Centerline Rd, near the airport. Tel: (340) 692 2280. Open: Mon–Fri 9–11.30am & 1–4.15pm.

US Virgin Islands

Yachts off Caneel Bay, on the northwest coast of St John, US Virgin Islands

Trunk Bay, St John, is rated one of the top ten beaches in the world

Frederiksted

St Croix's second town, Frederiksted, runs along two streets from Fort Frederik. Pretty stone arcades topped with gingerbread decoration protect passers-by from the sun's glare.

Fort Frederik

Blood-red Fort Frederik, which dates back to 1760, was destroyed by fire in 1878, and restored in Victorian style, and now houses a well-displayed and informative museum covering island history and culture, with a good section on hurricanes. In 1776, the new American flag received its first foreign salute from the cannons of Fort Frederik. Today, the 18th-century battlement weaponry lies silent.
Tel: (340) 772 2021. Open: Mon–Fri 8.30am–4pm. Donations accepted.

St Croix LEAP

Here in St Croix's mini 'rainforest', craftsmen at the St Croix LEAP (Life Experience Achievement Program) fashion all sorts of craft items from free-form sculptures to walking sticks, and fridge magnets from mahogany, saman and thibet wood.
Mahogany Rd, Route 76.
Tel: (340) 772 0421. Open: daily 9am–5pm.

St George Village Botanical Garden

On a 6.5ha (16 acre) site where Arawak Indians once set up camp and the Danes operated a sugar mill from 1733 to 1917, this botanical garden showcases over 800 species of tropical plants. A circuit of the gardens, which are attractively laid out among the ruins of the old plantation buildings, takes around 40 minutes. There is

plenty to admire, including orchid and fern houses, a fragrant frangipani walk and a rainforest trail.
Centerline Rd, near Frederiksted. Tel: (340) 692 2874. Open: daily 9am–5pm. Admission charge.

Whim Great House and Museum
Don't miss this gracious 18th-century house with 1m (3ft) thick walls and an air moat designed to keep the cellar cool. The unusual oval-shaped interior has been restored with period colonial furnishings and paintings. In the grounds, the sugar estate's old windmill and cane crushers can be seen.
Centerline Rd. Tel: (340) 772 0598. Open: guided tours Mon–Sat 10am–4pm. Admission charge.

ST JOHN
A short boat ride from St Thomas, St John is one of the best-preserved islands in the Caribbean. In 1956, two-thirds of the island was given by owner Laurence Rockefeller to the National Parks Service, since when the land-based portion of the 5,220ha (12,900 acre) preserve has been returned to its natural forest state. Around 2,265ha (5,600 acres) of the park lie under water off the north coast. Most visitors to the island are day trippers; there are frequent daily ferry sailings from Charlotte Amalie and Red Hook (St Thomas) to Cruz Bay. The visitors' centre near the Cruz Bay ferry dock has information about the park and its 22 walking trails, which range from 10 minutes to a couple of hours in length.
St John's best beaches are in the north. Trunk Bay, rated among National Geographic's top ten beaches, has snack facilities, snorkel hire and an underwater trail.

Cruz Bay, St John

ST THOMAS

When Dutch planters and the Danish West India Company first set up shop on St Thomas in the 1670s, the harbour settlement outside the walls of Fort Christian was known as Taphus, literally 'tap house', and it was a welcome watering hole for Caribbean merchants. Taphus was rechristened Charlotte Amalie in 1691, in honour of the Danish queen. Before long, the dockside waterhouses were piled high with goods from around the world, a tradition which has continued right through to the present day – though the contents are now Japanese electronics, French perfumes and designer fashions rather than rum, guns, indigo and cotton.

St Thomas Tourism Division Visitors' Bureau

PO Box 6400, Charlotte Amalie, 00804 USVI. Tel: (340) 774 8784; www.usvi.net

Charlotte Amalie

A pretty waterfront town clambering back into the hills from the mercantile mayhem on Main Street, Charlotte Amalie is a major cruise ship destination, servicing up to ten ships a day. The downtown area is a shrine to duty-free shopping, but if you prefer a breath of fresh air, and a taste of the town's history, take a stroll up Government Hill to explore the quiet streets of 19th-century public buildings and hotels linked by flights of steps.

Charlotte Amalie is one of the top shopping spots in the Caribbean

Blackbeard's Castle

The most famous of Charlotte Amalie's flights of stairs is the '99 Steps' which lead up to the commanding lookout point known as Blackbeard's Castle. Local legend claims the ferocious pirate maintained a base on the island in the 1690s and early 1700s. His days of lacing rum with gunpowder and splicing his beard with burning charges before going into battle ended when his ship, the *Queen Anne's Revenge*, was captured by Lieutenant Robert Maynard of the Royal Navy in 1718, and Blackbeard was killed in the fight. There are also several possible excursions beyond the capital.

St Thomas Skyride

A great way to get a panoramic view of downtown, the harbour and the offshore islands, these cable-car trams take you

up Flag Hill to Paradise Point, where there are nature trails and bird shows.
9617 Estate St. Open: Thur–Mon 9am–5pm, Tue 9am–7pm, Wed 9am–9pm. Admission charge.

Atlantis Submarines

This is a great way to appreciate the wonders and surprises of the marine world along the 2.5km (1½ mile) stretch of Buck Island Reef without getting wet. The hugely popular Atlantis Submarine dives reach a depth of 27m (90ft) beneath the surface, and experienced divers keep up a running commentary during the dive.
Open: daily, with frequent departures hourly from Havensight Mall. Reservations necessary, booking ahead through the cruise line is recommended. Tel: (340) 776 5650.

Coral World Marine Park and Underwater Observatory

An alternative introduction to the marine world, this small but effective complex features a 365,000-litre (80,000-gallon) reef tank and 'predator' tanks, as well as the 'Sea Trek' underwater walk. Check out the fish feeding schedules for additional action. The park also offers changing facilities and showers for visitors who want to relax on neighbouring Coki Beach.
*4km (2½ miles) northeast of Charlotte Amalie. Tel: (340) 775 1555; www.coralworldvi.com.
Open: daily 9am–5pm.
Admission charge.*

Estate St Peter Great House and Botanical Gardens

The outstanding feature of this contemporary great house is its fabulous views. From the observation deck at 305m (1,000ft) above sea level you can see 20 other islands. Take a stroll around the gardens, where more than 500 varieties of plants flourish and tour the exhibition of local artists' work.
3km (2 miles) north of Charlotte Amalie. St Peter Mount Rd. Tel: (340) 774 4999. Open: Mon–Sat 8am–4pm. Admission charge.

Magens Bay

This fabulous beach boasts over 1.5km (1 mile) of talcum powder sand sandwiched between serried ranks of palm trees and limpid blue water. It features in *National Geographic*'s list of top ten beaches in the world (along with Trunk Bay on St John).
5km (3 miles) north of Charlotte Amalie. Admission charge.

The Frederick Evangelical Lutheran Church on Government Hill, Charlotte Amalie

Getting away from it all

Nature lovers will have a wonderful holiday in the Caribbean, where finding a quiet area of outstanding natural beauty is (as they say in these parts) 'no problem'. That goes for Southern Florida, too, home of the Everglades National Park and its 2,000-plus different plant species. After all, Juan Ponce de León named the land La Florida after the Spanish Eastertide Festival of Flowers.

Since the days of the early explorers, visitors to the Caribbean region have never ceased to be amazed and delighted by the beauty and diversity of the islands. Beneath cool, green rainforest canopies, in cottage window boxes and botanic gardens, and even along the roadside, colourful plants and flowers grow in luxuriant profusion. Caribbean land animals are quite limited by comparison. Iguanas, some

The exotic lobster claw flower pops up in Caribbean gardens and on flower stalls

of which can grow up to 1.5m (5ft) long, and a couple of rare lizards are about the most exciting things to see. And there are several types of inordinately loud tree frog, such as the Puerto Rican coqui, named for its mating call (apparently, the 'ko' sound attracts the females and the 'kee' warns off the males).

Everybody enjoys the flutter and thrum of giant butterflies and tiny hummingbirds as they flit from bloom to bloom, and birdwatchers are definitely in for a treat in this neck of the woods. Ornothological types will find themselves reaching repeatedly for their binoculars in the hope of spotting a rare parrot or some of the other brightly plumed indigenous island species. Rainforest preserves offer superb birdwatching opportunities, as do swamp and marshlands like the Black River in Jamaica, and the Caroni Swamp in Trinidad, where the evening flight of the scarlet ibis is one of the natural wonders of the world.

Most Caribbean islands boast nature reserves and national park areas, but on-site facilities vary tremendously from country to country. In more developed islands, parks may offer visitor centres with interpretative displays, helpful literature, marked trails and guided walk programmes. However, this is not always the case, and you are strongly advised not to set off into wilderness areas without an experienced local guide.

Neither does nature stop at the shoreline in the Caribbean. What better way to escape the crowds than to spend a couple of hours snorkelling among delicate coral reefs? There are snorkelling opportunities off most of the islands, where the only crowds come in shoals, and the underwater landscape is stunningly beautiful. Areas such as the Caymans and Dutch ABC islands offer some of the most spectacular diving in the world.

Miami and Fort Lauderdale

Allow a full day to visit the **Everglades National Park** from Miami or Fort Lauderdale (*see pp40–41*). The main entrance and Park Information Center (*Tel: (305) 242 7700. Open: daily 8am–5pm*) lie 16km (10 miles) southwest of Florida City. The information centre shows an introductory film and provides brochures, maps, details of boat tours, canoe rentals and guided walks which depart from the Royal Palm Interpretive Center. The northern

There are more than 200 varieties of colourful hibiscus in the Caribbean region

entrance to the park is at Shark Valley, 56km (35 miles) west of Downtown Miami via the Tamiami Trail (US41). The Information Center (*Tel: (305) 221 8776; www.nps.gov/ever. Open: daily 9am–5pm*) can advise on trails, bicycle rental and tram tours.

Antigua

For some of the island's finest and least frequented beaches, head for the southwest corner of Antigua. Just offshore, Cades Reef is an excellent dive site. Nearby, Fig Tree Drive climbs up through Antigua's last remaining patch of lush, undeveloped forest.

Aruba

Getting away from it all in Aruba could be an equestrian foray into the *cunucu*, as they call the back country here, or a gallop along the sands on horseback. Both novice and experienced riders are welcome to join guided horseback tours from **Rancho El Paso**, Washington 44 (*Tel: (297) 873310*). Birdwatchers can

Dominica's lush rainforest quickly swallows up paths and trails

find peace and quiet at **Bubali Pond**, an old salt pan now set aside as a sanctuary north of Oranjestad, near Noord.

Bahamas

Nassau's **Botanical Gardens** offer a cat's cradle of paths, steps and leafy bowers, grafted on to the hillside below Fort Charlotte. On Grand Bahama, the 40ha (100 acre) **Rand Memorial Nature Center** boasts 21 species of wild orchids, nature trails, an aviary and forest ecology exhibits.

Botanical Gardens. Open: Mon–Fri 8am–4pm, Sat & Sun 9am–4pm. Admission charge.
Rand Memorial Nature Center. Open: Mon–Fri 9am–4pm (guided walks at 10am), Sat 9am–1pm. Admission charge.

Barbados

Start out at Hackleton's Cliff, a magnificent viewpoint 305m (1,000 feet) above the windward coast in St Joseph, and descend the path through **Joe's River Tropical Rainforest** to the ocean. The 34ha (85 acre) woodland preserve is renowned for its giant ficus

trees, stands of mahogany, cabbage palms and bearded fig trees (banyans) which give the island its name. On seeing the banyans' muddle of aerial roots growing down from their branches, Portuguese sailors called the island Os Barbudos, 'the bearded ones'.

Bermuda

Once upon a time visitors to Bermuda would have been able to 'rattle and shake' from one end of the island to the other by rail. Taken out of service 30 years ago, the old railroad has been given a new lease of life as the **Bermuda Railway Trail**. Pick up a free guide to the trail from the tourist office. It is broken up into easy-to-walk sections of around 3km (2 miles), and there is access from numerous points around the island.

Bonaire

Bonaire is famous for its flamingoes. There are two colonies on the island. The smaller one is in the north at Goto Meer. The **Pekel Meer Bird Sanctuary** in the southern salt pan is also home to many of Bonaire's other 124 bird species. **Washington Slagbaai National Park** occupies a former plantation site in the northern part of the island, and features hiking trails, caves and a representative collection of hardy native plants, such as cacti and windswept *divi-divi* trees.

Cayman Islands

Opened by its regal namesake in 1994, the **Queen Elizabeth II Botanic Park** features a well-marked woodland trail, swamp area, iguana habitat and ponds for freshwater turtles, as well as over 200 plant species. Keen birdwatchers can enjoy the Governor Michael Gore Bird Sanctuary, a 1.5ha (3½ acre) wetland preserve.

Curaçao

The 1,820-ha (4,500-acre) **Christoffel National Park** was created from three old plantations in the northwestern corner of the island. It harbours native deer, iguanas and rare lizards as well as many of Curaçao's 500 different species of plants and flowers. Within the park four short trails for walkers and cars scale the sides of the Christoffelberg, Curaçao's highest hill at 378m (1,239ft).

Dominica

On the western slopes of Mount Diablotin, the **Northern Forest Reserve** is an important refuge for two endangered parrot species. The 50cm (20in) tall Sisserou (Imperial Parrot) is one of the largest Amazon parrots with mainly green plumage and deep purple breast feathers; its more colourful cousin, the Jaco (red-necked parrot), is distinguished by a tell-tale flash of scarlet at its throat.

Grenada

La Sagesse Nature Centre is a former private estate in an isolated spot on the south coast. It combines woodland trails, areas of scrub cactus and

mangrove estuary with three lovely beaches and offshore coral reefs. On the north coast, the beautiful **Levera National Park** area offers trails, beaches and snorkelling. It's busy at weekends, but virtually deserted during the week.

Guadeloupe

The 772km (480 miles) of marked trails wend their way around the 30,350ha (75,000 acre) **Parc Naturel** on Basse-Terre. The Maison du Parc on the Route de la Traversée is a good starting point for excursions into the rainforest (*see p90*). One trail makes an exciting crossing of the Bras David River via a wooden suspension bridge.

Jamaica

Jamaica is a natural wonderland with marvellous birdlife. The national bird is the doctor bird, or red-billed streamertail, a busybody little emerald-coloured hummingbird which zips around local gardens. Jamaica boasts more than 250 species of bird, about 25 of which are endemic. A strange but true story: the hero of Jamaican resident Ian Fleming's best-selling books was named after the author of *Birds of the West Indies*, James Bond.

A great place to get to grips with Jamaican birdlife is the **Rocklands Bird Feeding Station** at Anchovy, within easy reach of Montego Bay (*see p96*). At Black River, in the southwest of the island, 90-minute boat rides explore the mangrove swamp area known as the **Great Morass**. An expert guide points out birds, basking crocodiles and other wildlife. **Black River Safaris** *depart daily at 9am, 11am, 12.30pm, 2pm and 4pm.* On the road south, stop off to visit the lovely **YS Falls**. These unspoilt cascades and pools are some of the most beautiful on the island. Bring a swimming costume.

Martinique

North of Le Morne Rouge, near the little village of Ajoupa-Bouillon, is the narrow ravine of the **Gorges de la Falaise**, carved from the volcanic flank of Mt Pelée by the Falaise River. During the winter months you can walk up the riverbed to a set of falls. Nearby, at **Les Ombrages**, there is a shady botanical trail through a well-watered ravine fed by springs and waterfalls, plus a *boo kai*, or traditional Martiniquan kitchen garden.

Puerto Rico

It rains 350 days a year on Puerto Rico's **El Yunque Caribbean Rainforest**, but for nature lovers this is one of the most spectacular sights in the Caribbean

Safari boats explore Jamaica's Black River and 'Great Morass' swamp

(see p113). A variety of trails sets out from the visitors' centre following gushing mountain streams, past explosions of bromeliads, hibiscus and stooks of bamboo over 61m (200ft) high.

St Croix

St Croix's 6ha (15 acre) patch of semi-rainforest lies east of Frederiksted, bisected by the Mahogany Road. Trails and vehicle tracks criss-cross beneath 30m (100ft) tall mahogany trees surrounded by lush ferns and invaded by bromeliads.

St John/St Thomas

The **St John National Park** is one of the natural treasures of the Caribbean. Hire a jeep, strike out on foot or join a guided walk from the National Park Service headquarters in Cruz Bay. Horseback tours can be made with Carolina Corral, Coral Bay (*Tel: (340) 693 5778*). A highlight is the **Estate Annaberg Plantation** ruins on the central north coast.

St Kitt's and Nevis

It is a full day trip to **Mount Liamuiga** crater lake, set in St Kitt's' highest peak (1,156m/3,792ft), and the paths are not easy to follow without a guide, but it's definitely worth the effort. Shorter trips can also be made into the rainforest. **Kriss Tours** (*Tel: (869) 465 4042*) arrange full- and half-day guided hiking tours. For something less strenuous, **Nevis Equestrian Centre** (*Tel: (869) 469 8118;*

www.*ridenevis.com*) offers beach gallops and horseback tours in the mountains.

St Lucia

East of Soufrière, the rainforest backbone of St Lucia offers some lovely walks and fine views back to the **Pitons**. North of Castries, the Forestry Division maintains the short **Union Nature Trail**, together with a mini zoo and a herb garden. Call ahead (*Tel: (758) 450 2231*).

St Martin/Sint Maarten

It is not easy to get away from it all on this tiny island, but the northwestern corner is markedly less developed, and there are a few footpaths for determined explorers.

St Thomas

See St John, *p148*.

St Vincent

The best hike on St Vincent is the three-hour trek up **Soufrière**, but with limited time the **Vermont Nature Trails**, just outside Kingstown on the Leeward coast, are more accessible. This is good birdwatching territory, and you may even spot the rare St Vincent parrot.

Tortola

The **Sage Mountain National Park** offers two interesting diversions off the main trail. One cuts through semi-rainforest, while the other leads via a 20-year-old mahogany plantation to a lookout at 521m (1,710ft) above sea level – the highest point in the Virgin Islands.

Trinidad and Tobago

Trinidad's spectacular birdlife and flora are legendary. The island boasts around 425 species of birds (both permanent residents and winter visitors), plus over 2,200 different species of flowering plants and trees. The best place to enjoy an overview of this is the **Asa Wright Nature Centre** (*see pp131–2*). If time permits, be sure to catch the dusk return of the scarlet ibis from the feeding grounds to their roosts in the **Caroni Bird Sanctuary** (*see pp132–3*). For details of the **Tobago Forest Reserve**, *see p137*.

Getting away from it all

Crocodiles can be difficult to spot as they float log-like around the shallows

Rainforest

The rainforest is the richest type of habitat on the surface of the earth, a veritable treasury of plant and animal life. Just 10sq km (4sq miles) of rainforest may contain up to 750 species of trees, 1,000-plus varieties of smaller flowering plants, 400 species of birds, 125 types of mammal and 150 different butterflies and moths.

All it asks in return is an annual rainfall in excess of 1.8m (70 inches) and relatively high temperatures with little seasonal variation.

When Columbus first arrived in the Caribbean, almost every island was covered in primeval rainforest. But within a few hundred years, European settlers had cleared vast tracts for their

Tree ferns are only one of the many species of trees in the Caribbean rainforest

plantations, leaving the flatter islands, such as Antigua, virtually bare. Mountainous islands, such as the Windwards, Jamaica and Puerto Rico, were more fortunate, their inaccessible volcanic uplands proving more than a match for the sugar barons.

The Caribbean rainforest is not as well-stocked with wildlife as, say, the Amazon, but is still fascinating. The framework of the forest is provided by mahogany, gommier and other massive trees which grow over 30m (100ft) tall to form a dense canopy. In the cool gloom below, lianas (climbing plants) scramble up towards the light, and the vast green cavern is festooned with ferns, mosses, orchids and bromeliads growing out of tree trunks and branches. Although they are attached to a host, these epiphytes (air plants) are non-parasitic, and survive by gathering water and nutrients which run down the bark. Some countries, such as St Lucia, Tobago and Guadeloupe, have taken steps to protect their remaining rainforests, by making them into reserves and parks. Tourism and development in such areas is carefully regulated to save those national treasures – but, even here, these precious stands suffer not only from industrial development but the perils of nature. In 1994, for example, Hurricane Ivan decimated the rainforest of Grenada.

The exotic ginger plant

Visiting the rainforest is a wonderful experience, but it is recommended that you take a guide if venturing off the beaten track. As well as providing plenty of anecdotes, local guides can spot the 'unseen' – from a rare parrot to tree frog tadpoles swimming in a bromeliad water reservoir. Hikers should dress sensibly in sturdy boots and loose-fitting cotton clothes. Improbable as it may seem when you are down by the beach, it can get quite chilly at higher altitudes, so take a light sweater or waterproof if you are heading for the mountains.

Shopping

For many holiday-makers, shopping in new and exotic locations rates as their most popular holiday pursuit. This will come as no surprise to the storekeepers of the Caribbean, who welcome the souvenir-hungry tide of visiting shopaholics with open arms and some notable bargains. Several Caribbean cruise destinations, such as St Thomas and St Martin, are duty-free ports offering the promise of 25 to 50 per cent savings against US prices on some luxury goods. However, it pays to know the prices back home before splashing out.

On other islands, duty-free stores, often conveniently located right by the cruise-ship pier, do a roaring trade in luxury items such as cameras, jewellery and perfumes. For something with a touch of more local flavour, check out boutiques selling Caribbean-style fashions in lovely bright cotton designs, or trawl the numerous galleries exhibiting local arts and crafts. Exuberant Caribbean markets are fun to explore. Piled high with exotic fruits, strange vegetables and knick-knacks, they are a great place to pick up straw hats and mats, beach bags and fragrant packages of dried spices.

USA
Miami
A water-taxi service from the Port of Miami ferries passengers to Bayside Marketplace, a top Miami shopping attraction (*see p23*). There are services to Miami Beach, where shopping spots include the Lincoln Road Mall, the galleries and antiques stores of Española Way (*see p31*), and the classy Bal Harbour mall. The Coconut Grove district offers dozens of individual stores and two mini malls, while Coral Gables' Miracle Mile is also worth a visit.

Fort Lauderdale
The smart boutiques and fashionable galleries of Las Olas Boulevard are the stylish shopper's first port of call in Fort Lauderdale. In the department store field, Neiman Marcus, Saks Fifth Avenue and Lord & Taylor gather in the Galleria Mall on E Sunrise Boulevard, near the beach.

Two other major shopping, dining, and entertainment complexes are Las Olas Riverfront and the vast Beach Plaza Mall, on AIA, offering a mix of well-known brand-name fashion stores and individual boutiques. Bargain hunters should head west to Sawgrass Mills, on W Sunrise Boulevard. This is claimed to be the world's largest discount mall, with over 200 manufacturer and retail outlets.

Key West

Key West's main drag, Duval Street, is a magnet for shoppers. T-shirts, beach and resort wear and all manner of crafts are featured here. For great deals on T-shirts, slip off to the T-Shirt Factory (*316 Simonton Street*), which offers outlet prices and multi-purchase discounts. Just up the street, Key West Handprint Fabrics (*201 Simonton Street*) produces a bright range of cool cotton casualwear, and table and furniture coverings.

CARIBBEAN ISLANDS
Antigua

Fresh off the ship, cruise passengers have to run the gauntlet of the modern Heritage Quay duty-free complex before reaching the streets of St John's. If you're looking for shopping with character, head instead for neighbouring Redcliffe Quay, housed in attractively restored wooden buildings. Look out for contemporary jewellery in The Goldsmitty, comfortable Caribbean-made cotton leisurewear in the sparsely elegant BASE store, jaunty nautical-style casual clothes in Wind jammer Clothing, and Kate Spencer's gorgeous painted silk creations and vibrant Caribbean prints in Kate Designs.

Aruba

A short step from the pier, Seaport Village offers an international collection of fashion stores, jewellers and other duty-free items. Several local stores specialise in typically Dutch souvenirs such as dinky porcelain gabled houses straight off the canals of Amsterdam, mini windmills and Delft tiles.

If you are on the lookout for the latest in clocks and watches, a visit to Caya GF Betico Croes, where Gandelman Jewelers stocks an extensive range, will be worth your while. Also, the Aruba Trading Company is a duty-free treasure trove.

Woodcarvings make a good souvenir

Cooking spices for sale on a market stall in Grenada

Bahamas

The islands' major shopping complex, Freeport/Lucaya's International Bazaar and Straw Market on Grand Bahama Island, is pretty overwhelming to all but the most dedicated shopaholics. Store prices vary from around 20 to 40 per cent below US retail prices, while bargaining is expected in the Straw Market. Another favourite shoppers' haunt is the attractively laid out Port Lucaya shopping and dining complex. Shopping in New Providence is centred on Nassau's Bay Street, an eight-block strip of duty-free stores, T-shirt shops and a Straw Market. Prices are similar to those in Grand Bahama, and vary very little from shop to shop.

Barbados

The Bridgetown Harbour cruise ship complex and downtown Broad Street offer the widest choice of duty-free

shopping in a range of boutiques and department stores. In Holetown, the Chattel House Village is an attractive shopping complex. The Best of Barbados craft chain has several shops around the island, including one at Andromeda Gardens. They carry top-quality local craft items and a range of gifts, from hot sauce and Caribbean cook books to flower and plant guides.

Bermuda

Tax-free Bermuda is an excellent place to stock up on life's little luxuries. The British influence is obvious in the tweeds and cashmere, the fine china and Edinburgh crystal. On Front Street, Hamilton, the three leading department stores are AS Cooper, HA & E Smith's and Trimingham's. Fellow bastions of impeccable taste include Archie Brown & Son (woollens), Crisson's (jewellery and watches) and William Bluck and

Company (china and glass). All the main stores have outposts in St George, and there are several pleasant shops in the Somers Wharf complex here. The Royal Naval Dockyard has an understandable leaning towards nautical-type gifts and memorabilia, as well as antiques.

Cayman Islands

Grand Cayman is a free port and British Crown Colony, so Scottish woollens, Irish linen, crystal and bone china are favourite buys. Most of the shopping action takes place on Fort Street and Cardinal Avenue around the Kirk Freeport Plaza. South of George Town, on South Church Street, Pure Art displays a tempting array of island crafts in a Cayman cottage. (Note that black coral and turtle products cannot be imported into many countries, including the USA and the UK.)

Curaçao

Willemstad's Breedestraat, Heerenstraat, and Madurostraat are renowned for the quality and variety of their numerous stores. Swiss watches, French perfumes, Italian fashions, leather goods, linen and liquor abound. Spritzer & Fuhrmann, the top Dutch jewellers on Gomezplein, also do a good range of china and crystal. Penha & Sons, *Heerenstraat 1*, fill the oldest building in town with other luxury temptations. For lovely linen, try New Amsterdam (*Gomezplein 14*).

Dominica

Carib basketwork and wood sculptures are the traditional souvenirs from Dominica. In Roseau, Tropicrafts (*on the corner of Queen Mary Street and Turkey Lane*) stocks a large selection of woven baskets. They also sell wooden parrot carvings, costume dolls and gift baskets containing bay rum, coconut oil soaps and spices. Another good place to find souvenirs is the Papillote Wilderness Retreat gift shop near Trafalgar Falls.

Grenada

Don't leave Grenada without a handful of sweet-smelling spices or without browsing through the local handicrafts. In St George's, a handful of gift shops on Cross and Young streets stock attractive batik items, basketwork, jewellery and carvings. Yellow Poui Art Gallery, at Young Street and The Esplanade, is the place to find local and Caribbean art, antique maps and prints. There are also several craft shops on The Carenage.

Dominica's Carib Indians preserve traditional basketweaving skills

Traditional costumed dolls dressed in bright
Madras cotton on sale in Guadeloupe

Guadeloupe

The Centre St-John Perse shopping
complex by the cruise terminal contains
a stylish French mix of souvenir and
clothing stores, perfumeries and smart
little pharmacies stocking toiletries
concocted from Provençal herbs.
Some stores offer a 20 per cent
discount for purchases made with
credit cards or traveller's cheques. For
more boutique shopping, head for rue
Schoelcher and rue Frébault. For
atmosphere and spices, don't miss the
noisy Covered Market.

Jamaica

Some of the best Jamaican souvenirs
are edible or drinkable, such as Blue
Mountain coffee, rum and the coffee
liqueur Tia Maria. The island is also
well known for its colourful tropical
print fabrics transformed into attractive
casualwear, and for its handicrafts –
from jauntily painted carved animals
and fish to pottery. The best of
Jamaican crafts are on display at
Harmony Hall, just outside Ocho Rios.
The Gallery of West Indian Art

(*11 Fairfield Rd, Montego Bay*)
concentrates on contemporary
Jamaican and Haitian paintings, but
also has a small but tasteful selection of
craft items. For serious shopping in
town, avoid the high-pressure touristy
'craft markets', and make for the air-
conditioned comfort of shopping malls
such as Coconut Grove or Island Plaza
in Ocho Rios, and the City Centre Mall
and Half Moon Village in Montego Bay.

Martinique

Stretching west off rue de la Liberté
and the Savane to rue de la
République, Fort-de-France's main
shopping district is crammed into a
grid of narrow streets, bristling with
French brand names. Chanel, Baccarat,
Guerlain, Lalique and so on are all
here, and some stores offer a 20 per
cent discount on items paid for by
credit card or traveller's cheque. The
jewellery stores around rue Lamartine/
rue Isambert are the place to find
Creole gold knot necklaces and 'slave
chains' which make unusual souvenirs.
Handicraft items are on sale at the
Centre des Métiers d'Art in the Savane
gardens; and Martiniquan rum is some
of the best in the Caribbean.

Puerto Rico

Calle Fortaleza and Calle San Francisco
run the length of Old San Juan,
forming two seamless stretches of
T-shirt and jewellery stores, fashion
boutiques, craft shops and galleries.
It is a browsers' paradise, with another

tempting selection of shops on Calle Cristo, where the Ralph Lauren (Polo) Factory Outlet discounts casualwear. The Centro de Artes Populares, in the Convento de los Dominicos, Plaza de San José, offers a full range of Puerto Rican crafts, leatherwear, jewellery, wood and stone carvings, hammocks and pottery including *santos*, little clay religious figures and Christmas cribs. For a terrific selection of Haitian art and folk crafts, check out the two branches of Haitian Gallery (*206 & 387 Calle Fortaleza – east end*).

St Barthélemy

As befits a duty-free port, Gustavia's shops carry a good selection of luxury items such as watches, liquor, perfumes, china and glass, but bargains are few and far between. The only local handicraft of note is basketweaving.

In addition to sunhats and carry-alls, bread baskets are a speciality.

St Croix

The best shopping is in Christiansted, around Strandgade and Kongensgade. Folk Art Traders, on Strandgade, stocks a wealth of colourful Caribbean crafts and some rather more unusual items such as jewellery made from larimar (a semi-precious sky-blue stone), amber from the Dominican Republic, genuine 'pieces of eight' (old Spanish coins), pottery from Puerto Rico, lignum vitae wood carvings and Haitian paintings. The options are more limited in Frederiksted, though you'll find several craft and souvenir shops on Waterfront Strand Street. The Whim Great House and Museum has a good gift shop (*see p141*). Another favourite is a bottle of St Croix's own high-quality Cruzan rum.

Shopping

Roadside craft stall, Jamaica

Local craft shops not only are picturesque, but can offer bargain buys

St Kitt's

Gifts, clothing and duty-free items are all available from the waterfront Pelican Mall complex, while up on The Circus, Island Hopper sports pretty printed cottons, handpainted pottery and wooden decorations, plus Caribelle batiks. For the biggest choice of Caribelle's popular cotton fashions and wall hangings take a trip to the factory and shop at Romney Manor (*see p117*).

St Lucia

The attractive new Pointe Seraphine duty-free complex right by the cruise-ship pier offers one-stop shopping for everything from a little black frock to a helicopter tour of the island. Bagshaw Studios have a branch here selling their colourful printed cotton designs featuring parrots, seahorses, hibiscus and other animal and jungle-type motifs, but it is more fun to visit their studio and shop at La Toc. For crafts buys, check out the Market and Noah's Arkade on Jeremie Street.

St Martin/Sint Maarten

Front Street, Philipsburg, is a duty-free shopping haven with great deals on all sorts of luxury items such as jewellery, watches, fine wines and leather. On the Dutch side, Shipwreck Shop is a good place to find colourful local crafts, Caribelle batik clothes, beach wraps and jewellery. Front Street also features several galleries. Guavaberry liqueurs are an island speciality, on sale at the Guavaberry Kiosk (*No 10*). On the French side of the island, Marigot has its fair share of chic boutiques and Gallic goodies.

St Thomas

Shopping in downtown Charlotte Amalie is not recommended for the faint-hearted. Over 400 shops are crammed into the area between Main Street and the waterfront, and they are packed with every conceivable luxury and souvenir item. Cruise passengers berthing at Havensite will find another fully-fledged mall at the bottom of the gangplank. St Thomas' tax-free status results in savings of around 20 per cent on US prices. For shopping at a less frenetic pace, Tillet Gardens, near Tutu, is a delightful artisans' enclave with galleries, crafts studios, a restaurant and pet iguanas lounging under the trees.

St Vincent and the Grenadines

Shopping is a very low-key affair in Kingstown. Artisans Local Art & Craft, upstairs in the Bonadie Building on Bay

Caribbean artisans keep craft traditions alive thanks to tourist dollars

Street, sells basketware and scented mats made from plaited lavender, straw art and handpainted clothing. Noah's Arkade (*Bay Street*) also stocks Caribbean souvenirs. Voyager (*Halifax Street*) stocks duty-free items. Bequia offers more choice with a selection of beach-style boutiques selling silkscreen *pareos* (brightly coloured cotton wraparounds), swimwear and the like. Local Colour (*Belmont Walkway*) has some great T-shirts with unusual Caribbean designs, a small selection of sterling silver jewellery, arty cards and island prints. Along the waterfront in Port Elizabeth, local craftspeople sell model boats, and tie-dyed shorts and vests.

Tortola

Road Town's shops are cosily accommodated in little wooden houses on Main Street, and include the foodie temptations of Sunny Caribbee (guava jelly, spicy chutneys and wooden pots of West Indian Hangover Cure), and Pussers – purveyors of yachting clothing, scrimshaw, rum and other nautical stuff.

Trinidad and Tobago

Frederick Street, in Port of Spain, is one huge international bazaar. Here you will find everything from Swiss watches, Swedish silver and French brandy to Indian saris, carnival costumes and calypso CDs. For more basic shopping requirements, just duck into the Indian bazaars and fabric shops at the southern end of the street. Luxury goods can be found at the West Mall complex, Westmoorings.

Tobago greets cruise ship visitors with a harbourside mall at Scarborough. On Bacolet Street, The Cotton House Studio does a good line in tie-dye and batik fashions and jewellery.

Entertainment

Among the most hotly discussed topics on any cruise is the standard and variety of the on-board entertainment. Most large cruise ships offer a day-long programme, which kicks off after breakfast with activities from aerobics on the pool deck to mid-morning bingo. There may be a steel band to accompany lunch, a pianist at cocktail time, and an after-dinner show. Night owls can gamble into the small hours, or disport themselves in the disco.

Obviously, the type and extent of on-board entertainment varies considerably from ship to ship. A small cruise ship cannot possibly have the facilities available to a larger vessel. It cannot, for instance, even accommodate flocks of dancing girls for Las Vegas-type show productions, let alone stage them. The passenger profile also has a bearing on the content of the entertainment programme. 'Party ships' do not offer ballroom dancing or bridge lessons; cruise lines catering for a more sedate crowd will not go in for cocktail drinking competitions or limbo dancing.

When choosing a cruise, find out what the cruise company offers in the way of entertainment. What good is a pumping disco if you like to dance in the old-fashioned way? Children may be enchanted by Disney characters at breakfast, but not the adults. Is the swimming pool big enough for you? Check whether there is a fancy dress evening, too, as you may want to pack a costume. The problem with much of the on-board entertainment is that it can appear a bit bland. But considering the cruise company's near impossible task of pleasing most of the people, perhaps this is inevitable.

Bars, lounges, and showrooms

The ship's bar (or bars) is very definitely the focus of social life on board. The main bar may feature a pianist or a cabaret act in the evening to accompany cocktail hour or to entertain those sitting out the main show. There is usually a pool bar for drinks on deck, too. Except on luxury 'all-inclusive' ships, drinks must be paid for in cash or charged to passengers' accounts. If they are signed for (keep receipts), the bill will be presented at the end of the cruise. Prices are similar to those charged at a resort – not cheap. If the bar has been declared an 'entertainment-free zone', then the evening pianist-cum-cabaret act may perform in a lounge with its own bar. During the day, lounges may be used for port talks (usually a brief history and lots of shopping information on the next port of call), bingo and trivia games or other indoor group activity.

The main lounge is often referred to as the showroom or theatre. With a stage, lighting rig and theatre-style seating arrangements, this is the scene of the evening show, which can vary in content from an all-singing, all-dancing sparkly-costumed production to a variety evening featuring magicians, jugglers and comedians. This is the time when members of the cruise entertainments staff pop up to do a short turn of their own. There are usually two shows per evening, or the same show twice, playing for the first and second dinner seatings.

Casinos

Casinos are always closed in port due to customs regulations, but once a cruise ship sails into international waters the cards are shuffled, the slot machines jangle into life, and the serious business of on-board gambling gets underway. It is big business for the cruise lines, and several of them operate 'cruises to nowhere', aimed specifically at gambling addicts. Many ships offer a 'full casino' with baccarat, blackjack, craps, poker and roulette, as well as the usual slot machines.

Discos and dancing

Hardly a cruise ship puts to sea without a dance floor, but facilities vary considerably. All mainstream cruise ships have discos with a resident DJ who supposedly gears musical selection to the customers. Mostly this is modern dance music, but sometimes a Big Band or Swingtime evening might lure older passengers on to the dance floor.

Considering the choice of evening entertainment is crucial when choosing a cruise

Bathing facilities can vary greatly, so make sure you check what is available on your ship

On some 'party ships' the sound system, light show and special effects are good enough to bear comparison with the best land-based nightclubs. Some ships also have a low-key club where you can just about talk over the music, or dance to a band.

Exercise facilities

It is a fact that the average passenger gains around 2kg (4lb) over the duration of a week-long cruise. To redress this unhealthy situation, cruise companies usually provide a choice of exercise opportunities. Health and fitness facilities on a larger cruise vessel may run the gamut from a gym and weight room to a sauna and solarium. Some even include a jogging track. The fitness director will organise aerobics or stretch classes for groups of various fitness levels and advise on other physical activities. The upper deck is generally the place to find outdoor games such as badminton, shuffleboard, basketball and the like. On the pool deck, bathing facilities can range from the sublime (waterslides or whirl pools) to the faintly ridiculous (postage stamp-size pools crossed in three strokes).

Games rooms and libraries

For passengers who enjoy a gentle rubber of bridge or a nail-biting game of Risk, most ships provide a games room with card tables and a selection of board games. The library often doubles up as a venue for card players to meet, so a rowdy game of snap is probably not in order. Friendly tournaments can be arranged by the entertainments staff, and a small prize may be on offer. Shipboard libraries are not usually very extensive. There might be a modest selection of periodicals, holiday-reading type paperbacks, classics and reference books covering flora, fauna and other information about the region.

Movie theatres

A cruise can be a good way of catching up on recent-release movies. Around half-a-dozen or more films will be shown on a regular basis during a week-long cruise. Details will be listed on the daily activities programme. Some modern ships, or those which have been recently refurbished, have televisions and/or DVD players in their cabins. There is normally a movie channel and satellite reception of US and other programmes, plus a DVD library.

Shore excursions

This is supposed to be 'sightseeing made easy', but independent-minded passengers may feel shortchanged by these all-too-brief forays. Most shore excursions depart in a convoy of coaches from the pier accompanied by a local guide. Many only last for a couple of hours, so passengers wanting lunch on board can be back in time, thus the time spent at the various attractions is sometimes severely curtailed.

Children

Once upon a time, a child on a cruise ship was the proverbial lonely little petunia in an onion patch. The odd nanny-supervised tea party and a three-legged race around the deck was considered 'entertainment'. The rest of the time a child's role was to be rarely seen and absolutely never heard. Now, all that has changed, and junior cruisers have never had it so good.

In recent years, cruise companies have grabbed a significant slice of the family holiday market by offering a raft of tempting fare deals, special facilities and the promise of a safe and easily supervised environment. Most ships provide some form of organised children's programme, while others are exclusively family-orientated. When booking a family cruise holiday, it is important to find out not only what the cruise company offers in the way of activities, but also what age group these are aimed at.

Activity programmes

These can vary tremendously in content and in the frequency with which they are offered. Some ships only run children's programmes on days when the ship is at sea, or during the school holidays. Child-orientated lines such as the Disney Cruise Line offer a full daily programme of events for children and teenagers of all ages year-round.

Activity programmes can incorporate anything from dressing up as pirates for a pool party to computer games. Arts and crafts classes, quizzes and magic shows may also be on offer. Most cruise lines provide a supervised children's play area, and there may be swimming and sports instruction, too. Some of the best and most broad-ranging children's programmes are offered by Carnival Cruise Line, Celebrity Cruises and Norwegian Cruise Line. Premier Cruise Lines to the Bahamas offer tie-ins with several Florida theme parks and sail with a full complement of Loony Tunes characters on board.

SUN ALERT

Everybody has to take care in the hot Caribbean sun, but children are particularly susceptible to its burning rays. Make sure they are well covered with a high-factor sun cream every morning before going out to play. Top it up during the day, and make them wear a hat and cover up around lunchtime.

Babies

There is no reason baby should not come too, but parents would be advised to make a few enquiries first, as some cruise lines will not allow passengers under the age of two. With adequate advance warning (at the time of booking), cruise lines will provide cots, high chairs and other baby and toddler paraphernalia. Check if baby food and formula are available on board. Again, advance warning will do the trick, but nappies are generally not part of the service. Parents travelling with small children, or those who fancy dinner without the kids every now and then, should check the availability of baby-sitters in advance. Some ships provide a pool of child-minders for both day and night duty, either for free or for a small hourly rate. On non-child-orientated vessels, parents may have to make arrangements with a sympathetic staff member, or other parents.

Kids' cuisine

Parents of fussy eaters would do well to check out children's catering arrangements ahead of time. Most children would trade all the gourmet delicacies in the world for a fish finger or a hamburger and fries, and many of the more child-friendly cruise lines recognise this by providing special children's menus. As a rule, families with young children will be given the early dinner sitting (around 6.30pm or 7pm).

On-board pools will provide hours of fun

Sport and leisure

Watersports, quite obviously, is the name of the game in the Caribbean. But there is plenty for landlubbers too: fishing, hiking, golf, cycling, tennis and horse-riding are all usually on offer. Local tourist offices and their overseas branches have details of most sports facilities and special sporting events.

Cycling

On weekends, the French islands of Martinique and Guadeloupe are a blur of lycra-clad cyclists tearing up and down swooping mountain roads. Mountain bikes (called VTT in French, pronounced 'vay-tay-tay') can be hired for the day or by the hour on many islands.

Diving and snorkelling

Some specialist cruise vessels, such as the *Windstar* and *Sea Goddess* ships, are fully equipped with scuba and snorkelling gear, while others may offer snorkelling as a shore excursion option. Experienced (certificated) divers will have no problem finding dive operators offering trips on most Caribbean islands. The local tourist office will have a list. Snorkellers can paddle about off any beach to their heart's content.

The best dive sites in the Caribbean are found off the Bahamas, Grand Cayman and Dutch Leeward Islands. On Grand Bahama, UNEXSO (*Tel: (242) 373 1244*) offers 10 to 12 trips daily for experienced divers and an excellent short instruction course for beginners. Bob de Soto's Diving Ltd (*Tel: (345) 949 2022*) is a top operator in Grand Cayman. Try Pelican Watersports in Aruba (*Tel: (297) 587 2302*) and Curaçao Seascape in Curaçao (*Tel: (5999) 462 5005*). Curaçao Underwater Park (*Tel: (5999) 462 4242*) is a snorkeller's paradise with easy-to-follow trails.

Dive enthusiasts in Florida should contact: Diver's Paradise, Key Biscayne, Miami (*Tel: (305) 361 3483*); Pro-Dive, Fort Lauderdale (*Tel: (954) 776 3483*); and for access to the Looe Key National Marine Sanctuary (*48km/30 miles north of Key West*), try Looe Key Dive Center, Ramrod Key (*Tel: (305) 872 2215*). Another superb Keys dive site, and possible day trip from Miami, is the John Pennekamp Coral Reef State Park on Key Largo (*Tel: (305) 451 1202*).

Golf

Golf is an increasingly popular pastime in the Caribbean, and there are courses springing up all over the place. Many are attached to resort complexes, but most welcome visitors, and can arrange equipment hire, instruction and caddies.

During the busy winter season, it is advisable to make arrangments in advance, but even a last-minute enquiry may be successful as cruise ship timing often means playing during the hottest part of the day.

Grand Bahama has some of the best courses in the Caribbean: The Reef (*Tel: (242) 373 2002*); Cable Beach (*Tel: (242) 347 6000*); and Lucayan Golf & Country Club (*Tel: (242) 373 1066*). Other recommended courses are Bermuda's challenging Trent Jones-designed Port Royal Golf Course (*Tel: (441) 234 0974*); Golf de l'Imperatrice Joséphine at Les Trois-Ilets, Martinique (*Tel: (596) 68 32 81*); and the Carambola Golf Course in St Croix (*Tel: (340) 778 5638*). For sheer scenery, it would be hard to beat Mahogany Run in St Thomas (*Tel: (340) 777 6006*).

Florida is a golfer's paradise. There are dozens of courses in the Greater Miami and Greater Fort Lauderdale areas. Contact the relevant Visitors and Convention Bureau which should be able to provide you with a golfing guide.

Hiking and walking

Ecotourism is a growth industry in the islands as an increasing number of visitors quit the beaches in search of the 'real Caribbean'. Rainforest trails, mountain lakes and volcanic craters provide a wealth of stupendous scenery and a great opportunity to stretch your legs. Local guiding companies have sprung up all over the place, and their services are recommended for anybody keen to step off the beaten track. Without a knowledgeable local expert, it is easy to get lost. Paths and trails can disappear with alarming speed, washed away by floods or simply reclaimed by the undergrowth. Day-long hikes are often impractical for cruise passengers,

The Caribbean Islands and Florida Keys offer some of the finest diving in the world

as they tend to start at dawn, the coolest time of day, long before the cruise ships have lowered their gangplanks. But it is still possible to get away from it all on shorter trails and in the many national parks. Tourist offices can provide lists of guides (you may like to contact them in advance), and often carry information and maps covering short island walks or historic walks around town. Always dress comfortably for hiking. Sturdy shoes and loose-fitting cotton clothes are recommended. Always take a hat and plenty of water.

Horse-riding

This is a great way to explore off the beaten track. Local tourist offices will have a list of riding stables offering guided treks in the countryside, along the beach or even in the sea. Check whether the stable also supplies hard hats.

Sport fishing

Most Caribbean marinas harbour a sport-fishing operator or two. There is no mistaking those elevated lookout towers and the selection of whippy-looking rods lined up on stern designed to lure passing anglers aboard. Deep-sea fishing for wahoo, tuna, marlin, mahi-mahi (also known as 'dolphin' – not to be confused with the friendly mammal of the same name) and the magnificent sailfish is available off most of the islands. One of the hottest spots for the fishing fraternity is Grand Cayman, which also reckons to have the best bonefishing in the world, and devotes the month of June to the Million Dollar Month Fishing Tournament. There are over a dozen deep-sea fishing charter operators offering full- and half-day charters, all equipment supplied. They include Charter Boat Headquarters

Golfers have a choice of beautiful Caribbean courses

Big blue: windsurfing off the Bahamas

(*Tel: (345) 945 4340*) and Crosby Ebanks (*Tel: (345) 945 4049*).

Florida is also a big-time sport-fishing centre. Fort Lauderdale's Bahia Mar Yacht Centre is chock-full of gleaming charter fishing boats. Or head north to Pompano Beach (11km/ 7 miles), the modestly-titled Swordfish Capital of the World, where the Hillsboro Inlet Charter Fleet (*Tel: (954) 943 8222*) operates a dozen vessels. The Florida Keys are a magnet for keen anglers. Every marina has its sport-fishing charter boats, and barely a month goes by without a big money fishing tournament run out of Islamorada in the Middle Keys.

Tennis

It is not usually easy for cruise ship passengers to find a tennis court, as most of them are attached to hotels and reserved for the use of guests. However, check with the local tourist office for news of friendly resorts or rare public courts. Hotels may insist on players wearing whites on court.

Watersports

As a rule of thumb, wherever there are beachfront hotels there are bound to be watersports facilities. In major resort areas, waterskiing, jet skiing and parasailing (the practice of being hauled out of the water attached to a parachute behind a fast moving boat) are all part of the fun. Windsurfers, pedalboats, Hobie Cats, Sunfish and other small sailing boats are also widely available for rental through the hotels or independent watersports outfits. Yachting is a favourite Caribbean pursuit. Several cruise lines offer sailing or motor catamaran trips as a shore excursion option.

Food and drink

Caribbean cooking has few pretensions, but many influences. Aromatic pepperpot stews, Jamaican jerk (chicken or pork cooked over a barbecue pit), curried goat and vegetable dishes such as okra, callaloo soup (similar to spinach), fried plantains and breadfruit are all West Indian staples with an African influence.

In the French islands, there is marvellous Creole cooking, a fusion of French and African ideas; Trinidadians snack on *roti* (Indian-style unleavened bread filled with meat or vegetable); Puerto Ricans enjoy *arroz con pollo*, a Caribbean-influenced rice and chicken dish cooked in coconut milk.

There is plenty of fresh seafood including lobster, shrimp, crab, flying fish (excellent in a sandwich) and conch (pronounced 'conk' and also known as *lambi*), a rubbery mollusc served up in fritters and stews from the Florida Keys to Trinidad.

Fresh fruits such as bananas, mangoes, pineapples and guava ripened on the tree taste twice as good as they do back home. Be sure to sample lesser known but perfectly delicious fruits such as golden apple (often served as a fruit juice), and superb soursop ice creams. No visit to Key West would be complete without a generous slice of Key Lime Pie.

Drinks

There are dark rums, white rums, gold rums and spiced rums. Some are so strong, like Grenadian Jack Iron (160 per cent proof), they can even sink ice. And the pirate Blackbeard is said to have spiked his rum with a sprinkle of gunpowder. Rum is the basic ingredient of cocktail hour in the Caribbean. It is used in Planter's Punch (add fruit juice, a twist of lime and a sprinkle of nutmeg), piña coladas (add pineapple juice and coconut cream) and iced daiquiris (whizzed up with lime juice, crushed ice and fruit syrup). Wine is imported and thus relatively expensive in the West Indies, so most visitors stick to cocktails or sample the local beers such as Red Stripe in Jamaica, Banks in Barbados or the ubiquitous Carib from Trinidad.

The best non-alcoholic beverages feature local fruits such as mango, golden apple and fresh orange juice. Fruit punch is also refreshing, and do try coconut water straight from the nut, or sweet sugar-cane juice.

Where to eat

In the following list of recommended restaurants the star rating indicates the approximate cost per person per meal not including alcohol:

★   under US$15
★★   between US$15–20
★★★ over US$20

MIAMI

Joe's Stone Crab Restaurant ★★

A seafood institution, with 'early Miami-Beach décor'.
*11 Washington Ave,
South Miami Beach.
Tel: (305) 673 0365.
Open: mid-Oct to mid-May daily 11.30am–2pm;
Mid-May to mid-Oct
Sun 4–10pm, Mon–Thur
5–10pm, Fri & Sat
5–11pm.*

Victor's Café ★★/★★★

Old Havana-style place serving great Cuban food.
*2340 SW 32nd Ave,
Little Havana.
Tel: (305) 445 1313.
Open: Sun–Thur noon–midnight, Fri & Sat
noon–1am.*

Santo ★★★

Sophisticated modern American cuisine with an Asian twist, plus live music and entertainment. Noisy and fun.
*430 Lincoln Rd,
Miami Beach.
Tel: (305) 532 2882.
Open: Mon–Thur & Sun
11.30am–11pm, Fri & Sat
11.30am–midnight.*

FORT LAUDERDALE

15th St Fisheries ★★

Award-winning Florida seafood restaurant on the Intracoastal Waterway.
*1900 SE 15th St.
Tel: (954) 763 2777.
Open: daily
11.30am–10pm.*

The Cheesecake Factory ★★

Something for everyone, from eggs and appetisers to pastas and seafoods. And, of course, the cheesecake desserts – you can indulge in more than 20 varieties.
*2612 Sawgrass Mills
Circle. Tel: (954) 835
0966.
Open: Mon–Thur
11am–11.30pm,
Fri & Sat 11.30am–
12.30am, Sun
10am–11pm.*

Mark's Las Olas ★★★

Sophisticated Florida fusion cuisine. Dinner reservations required.
*1032 E Las Olas Blvd.
Tel: (954) 463 1000.
Open: Sun–Thur
6.30–10pm, Fri & Sat
6.30–11pm.*

KEY WEST

Pepe's ★/★★

Popular local diner with excellent barbecues.
*806 Caroline St.
Tel: (305) 294 7192.
Open: daily 7.30am–
10.30pm.*

Rick's Blue Heaven ★/★★

Hemingway once refereed boxing

Tasty local beers are brewed throughout the Caribbean

matches here. West
Indian foods.
129 Thomas St.
Tel: (305) 296 8666.
Open: daily 8am–10.30pm.

ANTIGUA
**Big Banana Holding
Company** ★/★★
Great pizza served up in
former slave quarters.
Redcliffe Quay, St John's.
Tel: (268) 480 6985.
*Open: Mon–Sat
11am–10.30pm.*

ARUBA
Iguana Joe's ★★
Popular place serving tasty,
reliable Mexican food.
*Royal Plaza Mall,
Oranjestad. Tel: (297) 583
9373. Open: Mon–Sat
11am–midnight, Sun
5pm–midnight.*

BAHAMAS
Café Matisse ★★
Laid-back but elegant
bistro serving delicious
seafood and pasta.
*Bank Lane, Nassau, New
Providence. Tel: (242) 356
7012. Open: Tue–Sat
noon–3pm & 6–10pm.*
Pier One ★★/★★★
Waterfront fish
restaurant with fine
harbour views.

*Freeport Harbour,
Freeport, Grand Bahama.*
Tel: (242) 352 6674.
Open: daily 10am–10pm.

BARBADOS
Pisces ★★
Caribbean seafood
served on the waterfront.
*St Lawrence Gap,
Christ Church.*
Tel: (246) 435 6564.
Open: daily 6–10.30pm
Atlantis Hotel ★★/★★★
Excellent luncheon
buffet, ocean views.
Convenient for
Andromeda Gardens.
Bathsheba, St Joseph.
Tel: (246) 433 9445.
Open: daily 8am–10pm.

BERMUDA
Carriage House ★★/★★★
International and local
cuisine at the attractively
restored wharf complex.
*Somers Wharf, Water St,
St George's.*
Tel: (441) 297 1270.
*Open: daily 11.30am–
3pm & 5.30–9.30pm.*

CAYMAN ISLANDS
Coconut Joe's ★★
Busy, lively bar and
restaurant, offering
everything from rum-
laced ribs to fajitas.

*West Bay Rd, Grand
Cayman. Tel: (345) 943
5367. Open: daily
7am– midnight.*
The Wharf ★★★
Seafood, continental and
Caribbean dishes.
*West Bay Rd, Seven Mile
Beach, Grand Cayman.*
Tel: (345) 949 2231.
Open: daily 6–10pm.

CURAÇAO
Iguana Cafe ★
Inexpensive place perfect
for watching the ships go
by as you eat. Seafood
and Dutch specialities.
*Handelskade, Purida,
Willemstad.*
Tel: (5999) 461 9866.
*Open: Mon–Sat
11am–10.30pm*
Bistro Le Clochard ★★★
Atmospheric dining in
an 18th-century fortress
jail. Swiss-French cuisine.
*Rif Fort, Otrabanda,
Willemstad. Tel: (5999)
462 5666. Open: daily
noon–2pm & 6.30–
10.45pm. Closed: Sun.*

DOMINICA
**Papillote Wilderness
Retreat** ★
Flying-fish sandwiches,
omelettes and salads on
the shaded terrace.

This typical Barbadian rum shop serves the 'national drink' distilled from molasses

Trafalgar Falls, Roseau.
Tel: (767) 448 2287.
Open: daily 8am–1.30pm.

GRENADA
The Nutmeg ★
A great place for a
snack or full meal.
Lambi (conch) is
well done.
The Carenage,
St George's.
Tel: (473) 440 2539.
Open: Mon–Sat
8am–10pm.

The Aquarium ★★
Beautiful setting on the
sand, and a menu that
ranges from callaloo
cannelloni to ginger
glazed lobster.
Pink Gin Beach.
Tel: (473) 444 1410.
Open: Tue–Sun
11am–11pm.

GUADELOUPE
Le Karacoli ★★
Great French-Creole food
served on the terrace at
Grande Anse Beach.
Deshaies.
Tel: (590) 284 117.
Open: daily
noon–2.30pm.

Chez Loulouse ★★
Good for lunch. Spicy
versions of conch,
octopus and codfish.
Reserve for dinner.
Malendure Plage.
Tel: (590) 987 034.
Open: daily noon–3.30pm
& 7–10pm.

JAMAICA
Pork Pit ★
Spicy Jamaican pork,
chicken, fish or sausage
jerk cooked on a bed
of coals.

27 Gloucester Ave,
Montego Bay. Tel: (876)
940 3008. Open: daily
11am–10.30pm.

Toscanini ★★★
Beautiful setting on the
porch of an old
Gingerbread house, and
authentic Italian cooking
using the best of local
ingredients.
Harmony Hall, Ocho Rios.
Tel: (876) 975 4885.
Open: Tue–Sat noon–2pm
& 7–10.30pm.

MARTINIQUE
Le Fromager ★/★★★
Items include grilled
conch, curried goat and
the catch of the day.
Route de fonds-St-Denis,
St Pierre. Tel: (0596) 781
907. Open: daily noon–
2.30pm.

Habitation LaGrange Restaurant ★★/★★★

Dine in the grandeur of a plantation set in a rainforest. This elegant restaurant is a gourmet's delight.
Habitation LaGrange, Marigot.
Tel: (0596) 536 060.
Open: daily 8am–10.30pm.

PUERTO RICO

The Parrot Club ★★

San Juan institution, serving great local food with an international twist, and offering live jazz some evenings.
Calle Fortaleza 363, Old San Juan.
Tel: (787) 725 7370.
Open: Mon–Fri 11.30am–3pm, Sat & Sun noon–4pm.

El Picoteco ★★

Set inside the grand Hotel El Convento, and offering 100-plus tapas dishes as well as more substantial Spanish food.
Hotel El Convento, Calle Cristo 100, Old San Juan.
Tel: (787) 723 9202.
Open: Tue–Sun 11am–11pm.

ST BARTHÉLEMY

Le Tamarin ★★/★★★

Delicious salads and innovative fish dishes.
Anse de Grande Saline (1km/0.6 miles). Tel: (590) 277 212. Open: daily noon–5pm, plus Tues–Sun 7–9pm.

ST CROIX

Blue Moon ★

Sidewalk tables and dining room in old Danish arcaded house. Good New World cuisine.
17 Strand St, Frederiksted.
Tel: (340) 772 2222.
Open: Tue–Fri 11.30am–2pm, Tue–Sat 6–9pm, Sun 11am–2pm.

Comanche ★★

Terrace dining and broad-ranging menu.
1 Strandgade, Christiansted.
Tel: (340) 773 0210.
Open: Mon–Sat 11.30am–2.30pm & 5.30–9.30pm.

ST KITT'S AND NEVIS

Fisherman's Wharf ★★

Waterside setting on a pier, and good seafood as well as a nightly buffet.
Basseterre, St Kitt's.
Tel: (869) 465 2754.
Open: daily 6.30–11pm.

ST LUCIA

Razmataz ★/★★

This Indian restaurant is a welcome addition to the island cuisine.
Rodney Bay Marina.
Tel: (758) 452 9800.
Open: Wed–Mon 5pm–11pm.

Green Parrot ★★

French and Creole menu plus salads, and grand views from the terrace.
Morne Fortune, Castries.
Tel: (758) 452 3399.
Open: daily 7am–midnight.

ST MARTIN/SINT MAARTEN

La Vie en Rose ★/★★★

Elaborate dinners in this 1920s style restaurant.
Bld de France at rue de la République, Marigot.
Tel: (590) 87 54 42. Open: Mon–Sat noon–3pm & 6.30–10pm.

ST THOMAS

Gladys Café ★

Chowders, sandwiches, burgers and local dishes served in a courtyard. Excellent fruit punch.
Waterfront, at Royal Dale Mall, Charlotte Amalie.

Tel: (340) 774 6604.
Open: Mon–Sat
8am–2pm.

Agave Terrace ★/★★★
A sweeping panorama
and superb cuisine,
including red snapper
with lobster medallions
and jumbo prawns.
Point Pleasant Resort,
6600 Estate Smith Bay,
St Thomas.
Tel: (340) 775 4142.
Open: daily 6–10pm.

ST VINCENT AND THE
GRENADINES
Frangipani ★★
Seafood specials and
snacks. Delightful tree-
shaded, informal
waterfront terrace.
Port Elizabeth, Bequia.
Tel: (784) 458 3255.

Open: daily 7.30am–
10pm.

TORTOLA
Pusser's Pub ★/★★
Full international menu
restaurant upstairs; deli
sandwiches, pizzas and
English pub grub below.
Waterfront Drive, Road
Town.
Tel: (284) 494 2467.
Open: 11am–midnight.

TRINIDAD AND
TOBAGO
Veni Mangé ★
Appealing local lunch
spot in a colourful old
house serving spicy and
delicious Trinidadian
specialities.
67a Ariapita Ave,
Port of Spain, Trinidad.

Tel: (868) 624 4597.
Open: Mon–Fri
11am–3pm plus Wed &
Fri 7–11pm.

The Blue Crab ★/★★★
A favourite with locals.
Serves stuffed crab backs
and an array of Creole
dishes.
Robinson St, Scarborough,
Tobago. Tel: (868) 639
2737. Open: Mon–Fri
11am–3pm.

La Belle Créole ★★★
Terrace restaurant with
lovely views over Bacolet
Bay, and sublime Creole
cooking.
Half Moon Blue Hotel,
73 Bacolet St,
Scarborough, Tobago.
Tel: (868) 639 3551.
Open: daily 8am–
10.30pm.

Food and drink

Waterfront restaurants at Philipsburg on Dutch Sint Maarten

Cruising and cruise ships

Gone are the days when the average cruise passenger was as old as the hills and as rich as Croesus. Today's cruisers come from all walks of life and every age range. Their interests are diverse and their expectations high.

Cruise lines have risen to the challenge in style. In order to keep up with the passenger boom and the demand for higher standards and better facilities, they are introducing new cruise vessels at staggering rates. Never before has the potential passenger been confronted with such a wide choice.

For first-time cruisers there is help at hand. Travel agents affiliated to CLIA (Cruise Lines International Association) and PSARA (Passenger Shipping Association Retail Agents) have specialist knowledge of the cruise market. There are also cruise agents who deal exclusively in cruise holidays, and they are often a good source of special deals and last-minute discounts.

Types of cruise

There are two basic itineraries: loop cruises, which start and end at the same port; and one-way cruises. One-way cruises tend to visit more ports, and spend less time at sea. However, a loop cruise from San Juan, Puerto Rico, can visit up to six destinations in a week. Just as today's cruise passengers are a diverse crowd, so are the cruising options that await them. The traditional mainstream cruise ships pride themselves on catering to a broad band of customers. They promise excellent food, modern facilities, a wide range of general activities and evening entertainment. Most incorporate some form of children's programme, too, particularly in the school holidays.

Themed cruises

If you are looking for something with more than mainstream appeal, consider a themed cruise. This is an increasingly popular sector of the cruise market. Themes cover a broad spectrum from the gently educational or cultural, such as cuisine or wine-tasting, to murder-mystery outings and sporting cruises. Golf or tennis cruises offer tuition as well as stops for a practice on dry land.

Family cruises

Kids love cruising, and most cruise lines love families. This is reflected in a range of special deals and child-orientated activity programmes (*see pp164–5*).

Discounted rates for children sharing a cabin with two adults start at around 50 per cent of the full fare, and then drop. Some cruise lines even allow children under 12 to travel 'free' (although air fares and port taxes still need to be paid).

How long?

As a rule, short cruises are more popular with the younger end of the market. Cruises lasting ten days or more tend to charge a significantly higher rate per day, and the average age of the passengers rises accordingly.

Cruise-stay holidays

Cruise-stay holidays provide the best of both worlds and some excellent deals. They are a good option for first-time cruisers, or for families who want to combine a cruise with a trip to Florida; for example, you can arrange to take a seven-day cruise out of Miami or Fort Lauderdale, and several cruise companies (or travel specialists such as Virgin Holidays) can arrange an impressively discounted rate for seven nights in a Florida hotel at the beginning or end of your trip. The main embarkation ports in the Caribbean are San Juan, Puerto Rico; Nassau, in the Bahamas; and St Thomas, USVI.

Types of cruise ships

Cruise ships can be roughly divided into four main categories: deluxe, luxury, premium and standard. Somewhere between the top-of-the-range deluxe cruise vessels, with an atmosphere similar to that of an exclusive private yacht, and the monster party ships plying the Bahamas route, there is something to suit everyone.

Cruising gives you a different perspective on the sights, such as El Morro Fortress, San Juan

A cruise ship docked on the island of St Thomas

Deluxe

Small and perfectly formed, the deluxe cruise ship is effectively a floating luxury hotel with a capacity of 50 to 200 passengers. Its hallmarks are gourmet cuisine, exemplary service and a high staff/passenger ratio.

Prime examples of this exclusive cruise class are Cunard's *Sea Goddess I* or Radisson's *Song of Flower*.

Luxury

Luxury-class vessels attract a sophisticated and high-spending crowd. They provide elegantly appointed and large cabins, all of which will be sea facing, and some of which will have private verandas. Standards of cuisine are extremely high and guests dress for dinner. Facilities vary with the size of the ship, but generally organised on-board events are infrequent.

The emphasis is on informal relaxation. Notable in this category is the *Radisson Diamond*, the world's only full-sized catamaran cruiser, which boasts a retractable marina with jet skis, snorkelling gear and a netted pool area between the ship's hulls.

Premium

The majority of mainstream cruise vessels fall into the premium class. They are owned by experienced cruise companies, maintained and run to a high standard, and offer an enjoyable cruising holiday with good food, good facilities and a broad range of entertainment and activities. Guests will have the opportunity to dress up for a couple of formal nights. At the top end of this category are Celebrity Cruises, Holland America, Princess Cruise Lines and Royal Caribbean, all of which have a reputation for outstanding food and service.

Standard

Standard cruise vessels are aimed at a more casual crowd. It is difficult to type-cast them as they cover a broad spectrum from the huge, modern party ships to rather older vessels with fewer modern facilities. Two things you can be sure of: confined cabin space, and menus which are relatively short.

Is big beautiful?

The size of a cruise ship is no indication of its place on the luxury scale, though it is safe to assume that the bigger the ship the more varied the on-board facilities will be. Similar to a floating resort, larger cruise vessels (700 or more passenger capacity) can offer a greater choice of public rooms, dining alternatives, fully-equipped showrooms and more polished entertainment, as well as plenty of deck space for pools and sunbathing.

The megaships, such as Royal Caribbean's *Explorer of the Seas* (over 3,000 passenger capacity) and *Freedom of the Seas* (4,375 passengers), are like dazzling futuristic cities afloat. However, with such a large number of guests on board, they are bound to be somewhat impersonal.

Smaller cruise ships are more flexible in many ways. Most notably, their shallow draught allows them to call at ports inaccessible to big ships. On-board facilities may be more limited, but what there is can be positively hedonistic. Cunard's *Sea Goddess* ships (116-person passenger capacity) are some of the most luxurious ships

afloat, awash with champagne and caviar, carpeted with Oriental rugs, and equipped with state-of-the-art watersports facilities, launched from a stern platform.

Sail-cruise vessels

For a cruise experience with a difference, there are several sail-cruise ships plying Caribbean waters. The most luxurious sailing ships are the reproduction four-masted tall ships, *Star Flyer* and *Star Clipper*, each carrying around 170 passengers and wind-driven for around 80 per cent of the time. The contemporary 'wind-assisted' Windstar vessels (around 150 passengers), and the French-built Club Med ships (around 380 passengers), have computer-controlled sails, which may not be welcome news to true sailing types.

Cruising and cruise ships

Elaborate buffets are a chance for the chef's team to show off their skills

Hotels and accommodation

Holiday-makers planning to add a couple of weeks or just a few days ashore on to their cruise can choose from a wide range of accommodation both in Florida and the Caribbean. Hotels, resorts and apartments come in all sizes and prices ranges, and there are particularly good deals to be found during the summer off-season.

High-season prices in the Caribbean start in mid-December and end in mid-April. Between September and November many Caribbean hotels are closed. Florida's hotels tend to open year-round, but most offer heavily discounted summer season rates.

Cruise-stay packages organised through a cruise line or tour operator will specify hotel options. Independent travellers can obtain accommodation lists from tourist offices, or consult a knowledgeable travel agent. Remember to check out local government taxes (6 per cent in Florida), which can add considerably to the quoted room price.

Apartments and efficiencies

Self-catering apartments or condominium ('condo') rental is popular with independent travellers who require flexibility. A minimum stay of three to seven days is usual. Family-orientated apartment-hotels typically offer shops, a pool, play areas and sports and dining facilities.

On the budget front, many hotels and motels provide efficiencies – spacious rooms with basic catering facilities.

Plantation hotels

A Caribbean speciality, these lovely – and often very luxurious – hotels occupy restored plantation houses dating from the 17th to 19th centuries. There are usually some rooms in the main house, but others will be in the grounds in converted outbuildings. The atmosphere is quiet and facilities limited to a pool, maybe a tennis court, and board games in the library. Most plantation hotels are away from the beach.

Resorts
All-inclusives

Increasingly popular in the Caribbean, all-inclusive resorts charge a one-off price to cover everything – all food and drinks, transportation, sports facilities, activities and entertainment, and even laundry and beauty treatments. The obvious advantage is budget control.

The downside is that by its very nature, this type of resort discourages customers from venturing out. Guests, therefore, rarely meet locals and lose out on such holiday pleasures as dining in real West Indian restaurants and exploring other parts of the island.

Couples-only

A slight variation on the all-inclusive theme, led by the Sandals Resorts chain, which has outposts all over the Caribbean. Most have good facilities, a range of entertainments and the ability to arrange anything from horse-riding to a wedding (best man and maid of honour supplied on request). Couples must be 18 or over.

Family

Most resorts provide some form of organised children's activities, while a number, such as Sandals Beaches, specialise in family holidays, offering a full daily programme of activities and events for adults as well as children of all ages. Trained counsellors, day-care and baby-sitting facilities, and special children's menus are all part of the service. Naturally, Florida is well supplied with family-style resorts, and Jamaica is probably the leader in the Caribbean.

Sports and spas

Some of the best Caribbean sports facilities are owned and operated by resort hotels. Florida's sports and spa resorts offer unbeatable facilities for golf and tennis enthusiasts. Health and beauty-conscious types can enjoy saunas, whirlpools, massage, diet advice and a wide range of beauty treatments.

Atlantis Hotel on Paradise Island, Bahamas

Practical guide

Arriving

British visitors and other nationals from countries participating in the USA Visa Waiver programme simply require a valid passport and completed waiver form (supplied) to enter the USA or the US Virgin Islands. Make sure that the form gives the full address of your first night's accommodation.

American and Canadian visitors do not require passports to visit any Caribbean country, but must have proof of identity, such as a driving licence. However, since 1 January 2008 travellers to and from the Caribbean, Bermuda, Panama, Mexico and Canada must have a passport to enter or re-enter the USA. Visas are seldom necessary for nationals of other countries visiting the Caribbean islands. Again, a valid passport will suffice.

Cruise passengers commencing or ending their cruise in a Caribbean country will be required to fill out an immigration form. These are handed out on board aircraft or the cruise ship. Immigration rules are strictly enforced throughout the region, and the immigration authorities will need to see an onward ticket. The accommodation section of the immigration form must be completed, or entry may be refused.

Ground transport

Where possible, arrange airport transfers through the cruise company.

Those arriving at Miami, Fort Lauderdale and Puerto Rico's San Juan airports will find taxis readily available. Most Caribbean airports have tourist information desks which advise on ground transport and taxi fares.

The journey from Miami airport to the Port of Miami takes around 30 minutes; from Fort Lauderdale airport to Port Everglades takes 10 minutes; from San Juan's Luis Muñoz Marin airport to the Old Town cruise piers is 45 minutes. At Miami and Fort Lauderdale airports, SuperShuttle minibuses offer a quick and inexpensive door-to-door alternative to taxis.

Children

See pp164–5.

Climate

The Caribbean Sea and its semicircle of islands lie in the tropics, so year-round temperatures remain high with little variation. Though temperatures can top 38°C (100°F), this is a rare occurrence, and the heat is generally tempered by cooling trade winds. Daytime temperatures in the Caribbean average between 26 and 30°C (79 and 86°F); night-time temperatures are around 15–18°C (59–64°F).

The coolest and driest months are at the height of the December to April season. May/June and October/ November are wet, though tropical showers (particularly in rainforest areas) can occur year-round. 'Hurricanes hardly happen', but if they do they usually choose September or October.

Conversion tables

See p185.

T-shirts are always in US sizes. Florida, the US Virgin Islands, Puerto Rico, and other US-influenced islands follow the US system of sizes; Commonwealth islands follow the UK system; French and Dutch influenced communities use the Rest of Europe sizes.

Crime

Violent crime is rare on the smaller Caribbean islands, but on larger and busier islands, such as Jamaica, Trinidad or St Thomas, it is unwise to walk down unlit streets or along the beach after dark. Petty theft is a problem. Do not leave watches, wallets and cameras unattended on the beach. Carry cash in a money belt or waist pack.

Violent crime in Florida has been making the headlines for several years, though, to a large extent, the danger is limited to a handful of non-tourist trouble spots such as the Liberty City and Overtown districts of Miami.

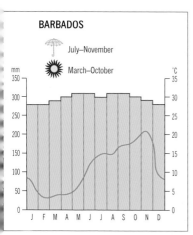

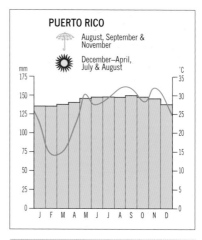

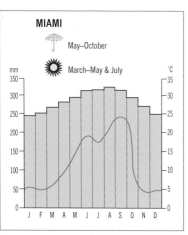

WEATHER CONVERSION CHART

25.4mm = 1 inch

$$°F = 1.8 \times °C + 32$$

However, basic rules of the jungle in any city advise you to leave any valuables in your hotel, carry only small amounts of cash and always stick to busy, well-lit streets after dark. If in doubt, do not walk; instead, take a taxi.

Rental car companies in Florida hand out a list of simple safety precautions which should be observed. In the event of an accident, find a well-lit telephone – gas stations, stores, or restaurants are recommended – and dial *911*. This call is free, even from pay phones, and connects with the emergency services.

Customs regulations

Alcohol and tobacco allowances vary from island to island. As a rule, the limit stands at around one litre of spirits and 200 cigarettes for every adult (over 18), as in the USA. Visitors from the USA can re-enter the States with up to US$800-worth of duty-free goods, or US$1,600 if returning from the US Virgin Islands. British visitors have an allowance of £145 on return to the UK. Foreign travellers departing from the USA within 48 hours are exempt from USA customs duties. It is important to remember that black coral and turtle products cannot be imported into the USA, the UK and many other countries.

Departure tax

Most Caribbean islands levy a departure tax on visitors. Cruise passengers do not pay this unless they are flying home from one of the islands. The actual amount varies from island to island, though in the Eastern Caribbean, it is around EC$40 (*see p186*). US dollars are usually accepted.

Driving and car rental

Car rental is readily available on most islands, but few cruise passengers with a limited stay choose to take up the option. In addition to a full national or international driver's licence several Caribbean islands also require drivers to purchase a temporary local licence (usually available from the rental car company), which adds to the cost. Check the type of insurance the rental company provides very carefully. Often the driver is liable for the first US$1,000 of any damage done to the vehicle. Some islands drive on the left, some on the right, and some are swapping from one system to the other, so check regulations carefully before you travel. Caribbean roads and drivers are 'adventurous'. Maybe too adventurous for a relaxing day out!

Car rental in Florida is inexpensive and easy. All the major car rental agencies have concessions throughout the state. Fly-drive deals can offer excellent value for money, and petrol (gas) is cheap. Driving is on the right. The top speed limit on the highway is 88km (55mph); on some sections of interstate roads this is raised to 105km (65mph).

Electricity

The electrical current in the USA and US Virgin Islands is 110 volts AC. Most other Caribbean islands have a 220 volt electricity supply. Cruise passengers with electrical equipment such as shavers and hairdryers should check with the cruise line.

Emergencies

In the USA, the police and emergency services can be summoned by a free call to *911*. In the Caribbean islands, the numbers vary and may be anything from three to seven digits long. Free brochures from the local tourist office usually list all the useful numbers on the island. Pick one up before leaving the main town.

Etiquette

Dress is invariably casual in the Caribbean and in Florida. Few restaurants require men to wear a jacket, and ties are almost extinct, though in the Caribbean save beachwear for the beach.

However, topless bathing is forbidden in Florida, and on all but the French Caribbean islands. However, it is unofficially sanctioned on certain sections of many Caribbean beaches.

Health

No inoculations or vaccinations are required for visits to the Caribbean or Florida. Tap water is drinkable in most Caribbean countries, but you should buy bottled water and avoid drinks with ice on less-developed islands.

Do not let sunburn ruin your holiday. Be sure to use a high-factor suncream and keep visits to the beach or pool deck short for the first few days.

CONVERSION TABLE

FROM	TO	MULTIPLY BY
Inches	Centimetres	2.54
Feet	Metres	0.3048
Yards	Metres	0.9144
Miles	Kilometres	1.6090
Acres	Hectares	0.4047
Gallons	Litres	4.5460
Ounces	Grams	28.35
Pounds	Grams	453.6
Pounds	Kilograms	0.4536
Tons	Tonnes	1.0160

To convert back, for example from centimetres to inches, divide by the number in the third column.

MEN'S SUITS

UK	36	38	40	42	44	46	48
Rest of Europe	46	48	50	52	54	56	58
USA	36	38	40	42	44	46	48

DRESS SIZES

UK	8	10	12	14	16	18
France	36	38	40	42	44	46
Italy	38	40	42	44	46	48
Rest of Europe	34	36	38	40	42	44
USA	6	8	10	12	14	16

MEN'S SHIRTS

UK	14	14.5	15	15.5	16	16.5	17
Rest of Europe	36	37	38	39/40	41	42	43
USA	14	14.5	15	15.5	16	16.5	17

MEN'S SHOES

UK	7	7.5	8.5	9.5	10.5	11
Rest of Europe	41	42	43	44	45	46
USA	8	8.5	9.5	10.5	11.5	12

WOMEN'S SHOES

UK	4.5	5	5.5	6	6.5	7
Rest of Europe	38	38	39	39	40	41
USA	6	6.5	7	7.5	8	8.5

Blooming marvellous: brilliant Caribbean flora attracts the birds and butterflies

Mosquitoes can be a real problem for visitors to Florida's Everglades and certain Caribbean islands in the summer season. Wise travellers carry a plentiful supply of repellent. Another potential health hazard is the machineel tree. Tall, bushy, and fond of a beachfront situation, the machineel has highly poisonous apple-like fruit and milky sap that can cause painful blisters and swelling if it comes into contact with skin. Do not even take shelter under these trees in a downpour.

All cruise ships have a doctor and some have infirmaries equipped to cope with emergencies. Passengers taking strong medication or with a condition that might require treatment during the cruise should inform the cruise line in

advance and renotify the ship's doctor soon after embarking.

Media

Most cruise ships have satellite access to American cable news. American periodicals are sold around the Caribbean. Internet access is available on almost all ships.

Money matters

The US dollar is local currency in Puerto Rico and British Virgin Islands. The common currency in the Eastern Caribbean is the Eastern Caribbean dollar (EC$) which has a fixed rate of exchange against the US dollar, as has the Bermuda dollar (BD$). The Bahamanian dollar (BS$) is kept at par with the US dollar, while the Jamaican dollar (JM$) and the Trinidad and Tobago dollar (TT$) fluctuate. French islands use the euro. The American dollar is accepted throughout the islands, although change will probably be given in local currency.

Credit cards and traveller's cheques are used widely to free tourists from the hazards of carrying large amounts of cash. Although some countries accept other denominations, Thomas Cook recommend US dollar cheques. These can frequently be used to settle bills in larger restaurants and tourist shops without the need to cash them first.

Sustainable tourism

Thomas Cook is a strong advocate of ethical and fairly traded tourism and believes that the travel experience should be as good for the places visited as it is for the people who visit them. That's why we firmly support The Travel Foundation: a charity that develops solutions to help improve and protect holiday destinations, their environment, traditions and culture. To find out what you can do to make a positive difference to the places you travel to and the people who live there, please visit *www.thetravelfoundation.org.uk*

Telephones

The Caribbean telephone system is generally efficient and easy to use. There are plenty of public telephones which operate with coins and telephone cards. Cards are recommended for making direct dial international calls.

Look for shade at midday

They can be bought from post offices, many shops, and information offices.

In the USA 'calling cards', readily purchased, may be used for long-distance calls. Avoid making long-distance calls from your hotel room to avoid surcharges levied by the hotel.

Country codes

Australia 61	**France** 33
Germany 49	**Ireland** 353
Netherlands 31	**Spain** 34
UK 44	

Time

Eastern Florida, the Bahamas and Jamaica observe Eastern Standard Time (GMT minus five hours). Bermuda and the rest of the Caribbean countries are an hour ahead (GMT minus four hours).

Tipping

Tipping is one of the 'hidden extras' most cruise passengers have to face. Some luxury cruise ships have abolished it, some have an optional tips policy, but on most cruise vessels tips comprise an important slice of the staff's income. It is customary to tip the dining room staff and cabin steward on the last night on board. Most cruise lines provide tipping guidelines, and a list may be left in your cabin along with envelopes marked with the name of the various recipients. As a basic guide, expect to tip the regular waiter and cabin steward US$3.50, and the busboy US$2.00, per passenger per day; the maître d'hôtel US$10 for the whole trip; and the wine steward 15 per cent of the wine bill. All

tips should be given in cash (preferably US dollars). Bar stewards can be tipped during the cruise.

On land, the attitude to tipping is fairly aggressive in both Florida and the Caribbean. Taxi drivers expect 10 to 15 per cent; the same for restaurant bills if service is not included. Tip bellhops around US$1/EC$2.50 per item.

Tourist information

In many cruise ports, there is a tourist office or tourist information point located on the pier. Staff will be able to provide maps, taxi fare guidelines and assistance with general enquiries about car rental, shopping, sports facilities, walking tours and hiking guides. For holiday-makers who would like additional information or accommodation lists before departure, many Caribbean countries have overseas offices in the USA and the UK, as well as head offices which you will find listed throughout this guide.

Travellers with disabilities

Many cruise lines are wary of travellers with disabilities and their attitude is far from encouraging. Others have modified cabins to provide a wheelchair-friendly layout. It is important to make enquiries well in advance of the proposed travel date, and supply as much information about special needs as possible. Contact a cruise agency specialising in advising on cruise holidays for travellers with mobility problems.

Index

Acknowledgements

Thomas Cook Publishing wishes to thank the following photographers, libraries and associations for their assistance in the preparation of this book.

PICTURES COLOUR LIBRARY 38, 69, 72, 97, 107, 109, 135, 141, 142, 177
DREAMSTIME R Goldberg 1, 22, 178, J Gynane 15, 154, K Chen 24, L Trecartin 36, Loulouphotos 43, B Howard 53, Slidepix 59, L Weslowski 99, 165, L Neeleman 108, 111, E Riviera 113, D Jackson 153, V Borilov 161, Alysta 162, C Opstal 167, R Verde Costa 179, R Sainani 181, S Nicholl 187
MARY EVANS PICTURE LIBRARY 84, 85, 104, 105
POLLY THOMAS 63, 94, 96, 126
THOMAS COOK OPERATIONS LIMITED 56, 57
The remaining pictures are held in the AA PHOTO LIBRARY and were taken by DAVID LYONS with the exception of: pages 11, 13, 41, 45, 62, 65, 77, 79, 83, 88, 91, 101, 116, 122, 125, 132, 133, 137, 139, 140, 143, 144, 146, 150, 151, 155, 158, 159, 168, 171, 173, 175, 186 which were taken by Peter Baker; pages 95, 148, 157 taken by Roy Victor; pages 23, 26, 29 taken by Pete Bennett; and page 149 taken by Jon Wyand.

For CAMBRIDGE PUBLISHING MANAGEMENT LTD:
Project editor: DIANE TEILLOL
Typesetter: PAUL QUERIPEL
Proofreader: JOANNE OSBORN
Index: MARIE LORIMER

SEND YOUR THOUGHTS TO
BOOKS@THOMASCOOK.COM

We're committed to providing the very best up-to-date information in our travel guides and constantly strive to make them as useful as they can be. You can help us to improve future editions by letting us have your feedback. If you've made a wonderful discovery on your travels that we don't already feature, if you'd like to inform us about recent changes to anything that we do include, or if you simply want to let us know your thoughts about this guidebook and how we can make it even better – we'd love to hear from you.

Send us ideas, discoveries and recommendations today and then look out for your valuable input in the next edition of this title.

Emails to the above address, or letters to Travellers Series Editor, Thomas Cook Publishing, PO Box 227, Unit 9, Coningsby Road, Peterborough PE3 8SB, UK.

Please don't forget to let us know which title your feedback refers to!